WARNING

This is not another get-rich-quick book. Nor will it give you the winning numbers to the next lottery ticket you buy.

HOWEVER . . .

If you sincerely want to learn how to program yourself to achieve your life goals, this book is for you.

If you want to be the best person you can be.
The best dad or mom you can be.
The best achiever you can be.
The best investor you can be.
The best business-person you can be.
Then this book is for you.

Study, learn, and put into practice the psychology revealed by Dr. Waldman and you will be equipped to achieve your life goals. The knowledge to do this is within these pages. But it is up to you to put that knowledge to work.

Are you up to it?

Too Busy Earning a Living to Make Your Fortune?

Discover the Psychology of Achieving Your Life Goals

Larry F. Waldman, Ph.D., ABPP
Clinical Psychologist

UCS PRESS
P.O. Box 12797
Prescott, AZ 86304-2797

UCS PRESS is an imprint of MarJim Books

Cover design by Marty Dobkins

Cover photo by Brandon W. Mosley

The names of Dr. Waldman's clients cited in this book have been changed to protect their privacy.

First edition, first printing, April 2013

Printed in the United States of America

ISBN: 978-0-943247-63-2

Dedication

To the hundreds of clients I have seen in my 33 years of private practice as a clinical psychologist. I appreciate the faith and trust they placed in me. While I always attempted to educate them, many of my clients have enlightened me, as well.

Acknowledgments

Special gratitude to Jeff Fagin, MBA, CPA, my good friend and hiking buddy, who inspired me with his drive, innovation, and entrepreneurship. He helped me to realize that most of the concepts concerning achieving financial freedom also apply to attaining life goals—and all stem from basic psychological theories.

Also to my friends Larry Beer, Esq. who guided me in staying on track and correctly advised me to stick with what I know best; and Cary Silverstein, business professor and consultant, for his thorough review of the manuscript with excellent recommendations

And to my dearest friend Harris Golden for his careful reading of the manuscript and his insightful recommendations.

Finally, I express major gratitude to the love of my life; my wife of over 41 years, Nan. Nan has always provided me with support and encouragement—in good times and in not so good times. Sometimes it amazes me how far we've come. It has been a fun run—and I hope it continues for a long while more.

Foreword

I am an expert in how people can change their thinking and their behavior, but I am not a financial expert. Therefore, in this book I am not going to provide financial advice, such as recommend specific areas in which to invest. Instead, this book is about helping people change so that they can overcome their psychological obstacles to finally achieve their life-long ambitions.

If I am not going to dispense specific financial advice, you might ask why I chose the title "Too Busy Earning a Living to Make Your Fortune?" I did so for three reasons:

First, like my four previous books, the title came from a client during a session and I liked the irony of the statement.

Second, I have become convinced that achieving financial freedom is more about personal psychology than understanding the stock market or earning an MBA.

Finally, the title conveys the frustration many people have. They would like to move forward but they can't, won't, or don't.

Many very intelligent people are eager to tell you how to get rich and become successful. Some of these wonderful experts have amazing insights and terrific ideas. I have learned much from many of them. The reason, then, I decided to write my book is that after reviewing quite a number of these books written by these experts, I have become convinced that nearly all of these experts do not possess a consistent, theoretical, philosophical framework.

As an adjunct professor of classes for graduate students who intend to become counselors and clinicians, I constantly remind my students that they must develop a solid theoretical perspective. When they are working with a client they must have an established theoretical reason to support what they are doing with and saying to a particular client at that particular time. Of course, therapists are free to choose the form of treatment they believe is optimal for a client, but once the treatment begins the therapist must be able to support what they are doing with that client according to a specific theoretical frame of reference. Therapists should be consistent and theoretically integrated, or the patient could become confused.

As I read many of the experts as they write about how to achieve personal and financial goals, they often are not theoretically consistent. While many of their ideas are great, theoretically they are, frankly, a bit scattered.

My good friend Jeff inspired me to write this book. Jeff and I often hike together on Sunday morning. He is so enthusiastic about the ideas he has learned concerning business and marketing, and always is eager to share them with me.

Jeff is a businessman and an entrepreneur. He has a business degree but he is not a trained psychologist. Interestingly, though, many of Jeff's ideas are psychological in nature. While hiking I would listen intently to Jeff's ideas and then I would reframe those concepts in their proper psychological perspective. In this manner we both have benefitted greatly from our hikes—physically and mentally.

My goal with this book is to educate you, the reader, using solid, accepted theories and principles of psychology, to help you understand why you are where you are, and help you learn to get where you want to be. Not only should you learn some helpful ideas to move you forward, you should also be able to understand from which psychological perspective these concepts originate.

Enjoy the journey.

Larry F. Waldman, Ph.D., ABPP

Too Busy Earning a Living
to Make Your Fortune?

Discover the Psychology
of Achieving
Your Life Goals

Larry F. Waldman, Ph.D., ABPP
Clinical Psychologist

About Larry Waldman

I was born and raised in Milwaukee, Wisconsin; the only son and oldest of four children. Although my father was a certified public accountant, money was always an issue; there was never enough. It was like the proverbial cobbler whose kids had no shoes. He worked very long hours in the effort to develop his private accounting business. Like the many mental health clinicians I now speak to, I have come to recognize that while my dad knew much about accounting, he unfortunately knew little about how to conduct an accounting business.

Looking back, I realize I was jealous of my first sister who was just two years younger than me and I resented that my father was gone so much. Desiring attention, I became the class clown in elementary school. I never really understood—then—the difference between people laughing with you and laughing at you.

I was bright—too bright for my own good, I now like to say. I was so intelligent that I got decent grades with little or no studying—which became my curse. I graduated from a demanding high school in the middle of the class with a non-impressive grade point average (GPA) because I continued to slide by on my basic intellect without expending much effort. I spent most of my time in high school working long hours—like my Dad—outside of school, to have my own car and fancy clothes that my parents could not afford to provide me. If I wasn't working, I was with my girlfriend. I remember my parents asking:

"Where are your books? (in my school locker)

"When do you study?" (never)

My father used to say, "It seems like school is getting in the way of your education." (He was right.)

Since I graduated high school with mediocre grades, I had nowhere else to go for college but to stay in Milwaukee, live at home, and attend school at the University of Wisconsin-Milwaukee (UWM). Back in the mid-60's it seemed to me that UWM was a small commuter school trying to find itself. You could not live on campus then. I was unhappy there, as most of my friends had gone out-of-state to school or had gone to Madison, to the University of Wisconsin. At least, I had my girlfriend who was a senior in high school.

Living what I had learned, I continued to work nearly full-time during my freshman year of college and, as usual, viewed school essentially as an afterthought. This was especially foolish, I realize now, as I was taking five-credit lab science classes, thinking I was going to become a psychiatrist. My first year of college I garnered an uninspiring GPA of about a 2.4, with 15 credits of C in science. I wasn't willing to admit it, but I had already closed the door on my dream of becoming a physician, as there was no way I could ever get accepted into medical school with those unimpressive grades.

By working hard (at my job) and saving money I made it to Madison (to the University) my sophomore year. I continued my pattern of working nearly full-time while attending school.

During the second semester of my sophomore year at the University I took advantage of an opportunity to serve as a research assistant for a young professor in the psychology department who was interested in the topic of learning. He shared his manuscript with me on how to study effectively—and it changed my world. From that point forward, through the remainder of my undergraduate and graduate education, I never earned anything less than an A.

As I approached my senior year I realized that with a Bachelor's degree in psychology "and a dime, I could purchase a half-a-cup of coffee," as my Dad used to say. I decided then to change my major to education—to teach high school psychology and maybe coach some football—so that when I graduated college I could get a **JOB.**

Since my psychology courses substituted for many educational classes, changing majors so late in the game only cost me an additional semester. That additional semester was my student teaching in Edgerton, Wisconsin, a small town about 45 miles southwest of Madison near the Illinois-Wisconsin border.

For most of that semester every workday I awoke at 4:30 am, drove to Edgerton, and taught four classes of high school psychology. At 2:45 pm I went to the gym, changed clothes, and coached the freshman football team from 3:15 to 4:45. (We had our eight games on Fridays.) At the end of practice (or the end of the game) I would shower and change back into my street clothes and drive back to Madison—at around 6 to 7 pm I would enter Ella's Delicatessen, on State Street, and work as the evening manager, closing at 1 am. (When things got slow late in the evening at the Deli I would prepare my lesson plan for the next day.) After closing, I would get to my tiny apartment by 1:30 am, fall immediately asleep, awaken at 4:30 am, and do it all again. Working hard was something I'd become quite familiar with.

Following graduation I had numerous offers to coach high school football all over the country, but I wanted to teach psychology or, at least, do something psychological in nature. I ended up teaching delinquent boys in the morning and pregnant girls in the afternoon in what then was the beginning of special education in Racine, Wisconsin, a small town off the interstate between Milwaukee and Chicago.

That summer of 1970 I essentially traveled around the world. I traveled on less than four hundred dollars for about ten weeks. It was a blast. "I sowed my wild oats," as they say, and I forever became bitten by the travel bug.

Near the end of that summer I re-met Nan. Nan and I had gone to the same high school and to the University of Wisconsin; we often said hello to each other but never dated. We saw each other daily for the remainder of that summer and I helped her move to St. Paul, Minnesota where she was going to teach fourth grade. I went back to teaching emotionally handicapped/pregnant teens in Racine. (I guess the District thought that pregnancy was contagious, back then.) That school year I tore up the highway most weekends between Racine and the Twin Cities. Nan and I became engaged over Thanksgiving in 1970 and we married in August of 1971.

I applied to graduate schools during my second year of teaching while I was engaged to Nan. Since my undergraduate GPA was not sterling, given the slow start my freshman and sophomore years, I got accepted into graduate school at UWM (again) and Temple University, in Philadelphia.

Nan and I decided to remain in Milwaukee. I accepted UWM's offer and Nan returned to Milwaukee and began teaching in the Oak Creek School District in South Milwaukee while I began my graduate studies in school psychology at UWM. (UWM had some dorms and was no longer strictly a commuter school by then.) Once again, I continued to work—as an undergraduate adjunct professor of educational psychology and as an evening and weekend child care counselor for delinquent boys (Witt Hall, on Prospect Avenue), while I attended graduate school.

Midway through my program I met my mentor, Dr. Karl Riem, as he taught a required class at UWM. In addition to adjunct teaching, Karl also ran the Special Development Clinic at Milwaukee Children's Hospital, was a consultant to several private boys' homes in the County, and also had an active private practice. Additionally, he was very well invested in commodities and real estate. I did a one-year practicum with Karl at the Hospital teaching parents how to understand and manage their developmentally-delayed children. Karl not only taught me clinical skills; he also taught me that as a psychologist you can help people but you can also become wealthy.

I graduated from UWM in August of 1973 with an Education-Specialist degree (60-credit Master's degree) and with certification as a school psychologist. Nan and I decided to move to the Southwest and settled in Phoenix. I became a school psychologist for Scottsdale Public Schools and Nan began teaching in the fourth grade for the Peoria School District, a western suburb of Phoenix. At the same time, while I was working as a school psychologist, I began my doctoral program in school psychology at Arizona State University (ASU). (I guess it was destined that I work and attend school simultaneously.)

Josh was born in 1976 and Chad in 1981. I loved being a dad. I believe I was a good one. My training and experience served me well in this regard.

I obtained my PhD in 1979 and left Scottsdale Schools shortly thereafter and started my private practice of psychology in January of 1980. Today my practice is one of the most successful ones in the Valley.

My practice is quite varied:

I still see children and parents, but I also work with adults and couples. Additionally, I have an active forensic (legal) practice in which I conduct custody evaluations, provide psychological evaluations for the Court, do parenting coordinating for the Court, and work with immigration, estate planning, and personal injury attorneys. I also have been a medical consultant for Social Security for the past 22 years. I teach graduate courses for Northern Arizona University in Phoenix. In addition to this book, I have written *Who's Raising Whom? A Parent's Guide to Effective Child Discipline,* in 1987; *Coping With Your Adolescent,* in 1994; *How Come I Love Him But Can't Live With Him? Making Your Marriage Work Better,* 2004; and *The Graduate Course You Never Had: How to Develop, Manage, and Market A Thriving Mental Health Practice—With and Without Managed Care,* 2011. I speak around the country on the topics of parenting and marriage and present to mental health associations on how to develop, manage and market a private mental help practice. Along with this—my fifth book—I also speak on the topic of achieving your financial and personal goals.

Nan and I recently celebrated our 41^{sh} anniversary. Josh, 37, is an attorney in Irvine, California and of this writing just married a wonderful young woman. Chad, 32, is a school psychologist in Portland, Oregon (starting out like his dad) and lives with a great young woman who I believe is absolutely perfect for him. Nan and I paid for our sons' educations so they did not have to work while they went to school. Interesting, how that happened.

Nan recently retired from teaching fourth grade for 29 years. She did a masterful job. We figure she had an impact on over 900 kids and families during her career.

I am 66. I have gone to the gym four days per week for the past 45 years—and I rarely miss a workout. As a psychologist, being physically fit is as important to me as being mentally fit.

I am fortunate. I was apparently blessed with good genes—the tendency to easily gain weight notwithstanding. I grew up in only a mildly dysfunctional home. I was also imbued with a strong work ethic and a desire to learn new things. I managed to work and associate with people who inspired me to accept change, overcome obstacles, and think creatively.

Larry F. Waldman

March 21, 2013

Table of Contents

CHAPTER ONE

How We Got "Stuck"

"If you believe you are a failure or a success, you're right!"

Henry Ford

As a clinical psychologist in private practice in Phoenix for the past 33 years, I have sat across from hundreds, perhaps thousands, of clients/patients who are struggling with problems in their lives. Many of these individuals are dealing with clinical concerns, such as depression, anxiety or mood disorder; or they may have a child with a developmental delay.

A significant number of my clients, though, are seeking psychotherapy because they have been unable to reach their financial and/or personal goals. These individuals are frustrated because they are trapped in a dead-end, unsatisfying, low-paying job that barely allows them to meet their basic monetary means and certainly does not afford them the opportunity to travel, recreate, or pursue a hobby. They are financially limited—trapped.

Many of my clients are unhappy because they have failed to reach some life goal—such as earn a college degree, become a nurse, try their hand at some dream job, author a book, have a successful relationship, and raise a responsible child. The aim of this book, then, is to help you, the reader, understand how you got where you are, why you are "stuck" where you are, and, using sound, basic principles of psychology, how you can move forward and begin achieving your personal and financial goals.

"Stuck in a rut"

A common maxim among mental health professionals is:

"Insanity is continuing to do the same thing but expecting a different result."

The reason this quip is common is that many people, unfortunately, do exactly that:

They want and wish for all sorts of new things and opportunities, but daily go about doing the very same activities that continue to bring them that which they already have—and may not even want. Despite their *dreams* and *desires*, they *act* in such a manner that brings something else—what they already have and are unhappy with.

Years ago I shared the speaking podium with a colleague, Dr. James Campbell, psychiatrist, as we conjointly made presentations to the community and other mental health professionals on various methods of psychotherapy. Jim usually did this vignette in which he referred to a baker who regularly went about the process of preparing a cake but when he pulled his work out of the oven he was always disappointed because he actually wanted pie. Nevertheless, the following morning the baker again followed the recipe for cake but, once more, was unhappy when he failed to produce pie. Thus, although this baker truly desired pie, as long as he continued to make cake, cake is what he was always going to get. Similarly, I have seen hundreds of clients who daily go about "making cake" when they dream about and desire "pie."

These individuals are "stuck in a rut." They most likely know they are stuck. They know they don't like being stuck. They may even know, to some degree, what they might like to do if they got out of their rut, but they cannot seem to do it.

Most people want to improve their lives. They would like to:

Leave their unsatisfying job and do something more creative, fulfilling—and lucrative.

Start a business.

Lose weight and get into good physical condition.

Develop a new hobby.

Write a book.

Travel.

Become a better spouse.

Become a better parent.

Become a better friend.
Become a better person.
Become financially independent.
And so forth.

Why we get "Stuck" and remain "Stuck"

The Need for Immediate Gratification

A major reason which causes people to become "stuck in their rut" is the issue of **immediate gratification**. As infants, we demand and expect that our needs be met immediately. A child wants what they want when they want it. When a child's needs are not satisfied immediately, he will cry and even throw a tantrum. It would be inappropriate, of course, to expect an infant or a young child to postpone their needs.

As the child ages and matures he/she becomes socialized to curb some of his/her natural impulses, like pooping in their pants, and learns to delay his/her gratification. Accordingly, by the time the child is about ten, for example, the child is told "big boys/girls don't cry" and to "save your money for a rainy day."

I believe that the mark of a **mature** adult is the ability to effectively delay gratification. This developmental transition from the infant's need for immediate satisfaction to the adult's ability to delay gratification, though, is more complete in some adults than in others. Some adults continue to struggle with inhibiting their impulses and prolonging their need for immediate satisfaction. For example:

They have temper tantrums when frustrated or angry; they spend their money quickly and foolishly, rather than save it or invest it; and they consume sugary, starchy, fatty foods because these foods taste so good going down, yet are ultimately fattening and unhealthy.

When you invest money in something, for instance, you are taking money that you could spend immediately and, instead, are hoping that in the future your investment will pay dividends. As a mature adult, you are delaying your immediate gratification so you may garner even more financial reinforcement in the future.

By the same token, when you invest the time and money in education you are investing the time and money you could play with today for the long-term reward of an education and a degree for the future. The time and money I invested in my education has repaid me a hundred times over, at least. By paying for my sons' educations I significantly improved the odds that my sons would likely be able to support themselves—and their Mother and I would not have to worry too much about them—at least financially.

When you eschew a hot fudge sundae for dessert and opt instead for a piece of fruit, you are also displaying some maturity. Unquestionably, you know that the sundae will taste very sweet and good going down, but you also know it will do you no good and possibly even some harm in the future (like not having their pants fit, among other problems). Choosing fruit over an ice cream sundae for dessert is an example of properly delaying gratification. The person who regularly chooses fruit for dessert over ice cream will likely be trimmer and healthier in the future. Though most adults *know* this, the immediate pleasure of an ice cream treat is too difficult for many adults to pass up—despite the possible long-term negative results. (I am not saying that once in awhile people cannot indulge themselves or have a treat. What I am referring to is the regular on-going food choices people make.)

Losing weight, for instance, would be relatively simple if you would choose to eat a healthy meal, then step on the scale and see it register a pound or two less. Unfortunately, as we all know, it does not work that way. To lose weight you must frequently and consistently choose to eat responsibly, thereby delaying gratification, and wait for the delayed reinforcement of a slimmer torso.

When my oldest son Josh was in college he called me one evening and complained that the business classes he was taking were too hard. I believe his exact words were, "Dad, these classes are kicking my butt."

My response was, "Good, I'm glad." Josh was puzzled. He suggested I should be more sympathetic. I answered him by saying, "I'm glad it's difficult, because if it were easy, everybody would have a degree in business. The fact that it is demanding makes the goal more worthwhile. Why would you want to spend four years working toward a goal that was easy? Think how proud you will feel when you accomplish your goal—especially when it was challenging."

Josh muttered something like, "I guess so." He then uttered a familiar refrain:

"This is what I get for having a psychologist for a father."

Obtaining your life's goals is challenging—and it should be. To be successful you must confront and conquer the issues of delayed gratification and delayed reinforcement. Those individuals who continue to choose immediate pleasure over long-term goals will most likely remain "stuck in their rut."

Losing 30 or more pounds, getting into great physical condition, or becoming financially stable will not happen overnight. Anyone who tells you that you can accomplish these goals, or any similar goals, in 30 days or so is simply being unrealistic—and probably is trying to sell you something. For that reason, I very much dislike the term "diet" because it implies a brief, transient change in your eating. To achieve these kinds of objectives you will have to be prepared to make permanent **lifestyle** changes.

If you ate only cabbage and drank only unsweetened ice tea for 30 days, you would definitely lose some weight; if you exercised like a fiend for 45 days you would start to develop some muscle definition (not to mention become really sore).

But what then?

When you finally got off that crazy eating plan and returned to your old eating habits you would most assuredly gain all the weight you lost from your foolish diet—and then some. If you also returned to your previously lazy, sedentary ways, any muscle you may have developed during your crash exercise routine would soon be covered with fat. Any permanent change in your weight, physique, finances, or relationships will require time and consistency over time—but it will be worth it.

National economic data tell a sad story:

Every month more money is borrowed in this nation than is earned. (I'm not only referring to the Federal Government, here.). This statistic indicates that every month more U.S. citizens put more money on their credit card accounts than the amount of money they take in. They continue to buy goods and services they truly cannot afford. Each month they pay the minimum amount due on their credit card and their credit card balance continues to increase. It is highly unlikely these credit card balances will ever be paid off—because the interest rate on these balances is ridiculous—18 percent, or more. When the citizens reach their credit card balance limit, most of them simply apply for another credit card—and start the process all over again. I have seen many clients over the years that are paying the minimum monthly balance on three or four credit cards, all of which are at or quickly approaching their maximum limit.

Clearly, many U.S. citizens are unable to put off purchases until they can actually afford them. They succumb to the lure of immediate gratification but then pay for their need for immediate gratification with an extremely high interest rate. An item of, say, $500.00 which is purchased with a credit card and paid off by making the minimum monthly payment, could take six to eight years to pay off and ultimately cost, with accumulated interest, about $3,000.00. This assumes no additional charges for late fees. It immediately becomes clear why credit card companies are making huge amounts of money and are able to withstand all the losses that they have to endure due to fraud and bankruptcy.

People in this financial predicament are simply trying to survive. They live paycheck to paycheck—and each month they get a little deeper in debt. Every month they pay those bills which are the most important or most delinquent, but they rarely can pay all of them. In time they will be unable to afford even the monthly minimum balances on all the credit cards and at that point they have to face some hard choices—like take a second job, sell some of their stuff, stop paying some bills altogether, or file for bankruptcy. Of course, if people in this financial situation experience a health issue, get laid off, or the transmission falls out of their primary vehicle, they are immediately in a deep financial crisis.

I read recently that several thousand Americans retire daily. Another sad statistic—recently cited at 47%—is that many of these persons who retire today have not financially prepared for retirement and are completely dependent on Social Security for their financial well-being. What will happen to these elderly folks if the government reduces Social Security benefits or scraps the program all together? Many of these seniors were unable to "save for a rainy day" or, better, invest, and spent all their income without preparing for retirement. For many, giving into immediate gratification ultimately sacrificed their retirement. Some folks may never be able to retire and many others will eke out their "golden years" scrimping from one Social Security check to the next.

To obtain a life goal they will have to confront and conquer these issues of delayed gratification and delayed reinforcement:

They might have to eat healthier and forgo pleasure/comfort food.

They may have to save and/or invest money rather than impulsively spend it.

They may have to choose to exercise, rather than veg on the couch.

They may have to carefully budget their time, rather than choose to "hang out."

They may have to work or attend classes or school instead of play.

They may have to stifle their anger and speak to their family members calmly.

When we make the responsible choice, progress, unfortunately, is slow. Getting in shape, earning a degree, learning to manage your money, or changing the nature of a significant relationship, all takes time. It does not happen overnight. Yet, with direction and perseverance you can do it! Just think how great it will be and how good you will feel when you accomplish your goal. Moreover, consider how positive your future will be with your new goal in hand. Achieving your life's goals unquestionably requires commitment and persistence. It will not be easy—and like I told Josh, it shouldn't be. It will require work—but it can be done. It will require **responsible** choices—on a continuing basis. You will have to act like the mature adult you are rather than capitulate to the child-like desire for immediate gratification.

Fear

Fear keeps many people "stuck." **Change** is stressful. Leaving behind your normal routine can be threatening. While the old routine may well be unsatisfying, it is, at the same time, familiar— possibly even comfortable.

We have all heard the old expression:

"What do you fear more: The devil you know or the devil you don't?"

Change, in and of itself, is frightening. Some people would rather remain stuck in an unsatisfying, unfulfilling rut because, at least, it is familiar. Doing something different and facing the unknown is scary. The fear of the unknown keeps many folks from making positive changes in their lives.

As the saying goes:

"People change when the pain not to change exceeds the pain to change."

Even positive changes can be fear-producing. Getting married, having a baby, buying a house, moving to a new neighborhood, taking a promotion, or securing a new job are all considered good, but yet they can be very stressful. Some people would rather stay in the old, unsatisfying but familiar position than risk doing something new and good—but different.

In addition to change, without a doubt, the fear of **failure** also serves to immobilize people. Having to make a success out of a new choice is doubly threatening.

"What if I should fail?"

How upsetting would it be to leave the rut—only to fail at the new opportunity?

I like the expression:

"Failure inspires winners and defeats losers."

Unfortunately, for many people a simple setback confirms their feelings of incompetence.

Stepping outside of your "rut" entails taking a **risk**. Changing your job, adding a part-time job, taking a class or joining a gym, all involve making a commitment of time, effort, and probably money. If that commitment results in a failure, most individuals are unwilling to take on another challenge and risk another failure. For many people, "the fear of losing money is greater than the joy of becoming successful."

Many of my clients have had first-hand experience with failure and would rather stay put than stick their neck out again. They have become conditioned to failure—and, frankly, expect it.

When the topic of change is broached with many of my clients, many essentially say:

"You want me to give up the job I have, my sole source of support, and strike out into the unknown and try to find something better!"

You can clearly feel the fear they are expressing. Fran Tarkington, the retired quarterback of the NFL Minnesota Vikings said," Winning means you are not afraid to lose."

Recently, I "brainstormed" with a client about the places and people he might contact regarding a particular type of work he very much wanted. As soon as I suggested a possibility, he would immediately begin to shoot it down. After seeing this for a bit, I noted to him that he was "closing the door on opportunities before he ever walked through any of them." I suggested he could "always say no" to an opportunity, if he has to or chooses to, but he should first explore every possibility he can. This individual was "slamming doors" on ideas so he did not have to risk the fear of failure, if he should walk through them. His deep fear of failure was clearly keeping him very "stuck."

When someone is in a survival mood, as described above, they are not likely to take chances or think outside the box. They are going to play it safe and do what it takes to survive one more day. It is difficult to delay gratification, take risks and think about the future, when you are concerned about surviving *today*.

This fear of failure causes individuals to refrain from venturing forth. The fear can be so pervasive it prevents people from even attempting to change. By avoiding the risk of failure you won't have to face another defeat, but you sacrifice the opportunity to change and get out of your "rut." Thus, the fear of another failure keeps you "stuck."

Even the fear of **success** stymies some people. I have had clients imply that if, by some miracle, they were to become rich and successful that would be really frightening, too. They noted that if they were rich, other people would have many more expectations of them, they would have far more obligations and responsibilities, and they would be expected to help people. Thus, once again, another fear keeps you stuck.

Your Financial Blueprint

Most people practice the same religion as their parents. Similarly, they usually follow the same political ideology as their mother and father. By the same token, they typically have prejudices and stereotypes consistent with those of their parents. These "attitudes" are values and mind-sets that we derive from the two most important people in our early lives—our parents or primary caregivers. We hear, observe, model, and learn from our parents as children and accept what we experienced from our parents as **The Truth!** What choice did we have? I have never heard of a three-year-old say, "Mom, Dad, I don't want to be a Catholic anymore; I've decided to become a Lutheran." Few of us, even as adults, challenge those precepts we gleaned during our childhood.

One of these attitudes we learned as a child and typically follows us into adulthood is our attitude regarding money. This is called our **Financial Blueprint.** As a child how did your parents behave around money? Did they often fight about it or were they in concert regarding the topic? Did they manage their money well or were they always in a financial bind? Were they miserly savers or lavish spenders—or somewhere in between?

As a child, what did your parents say about money?

"Money is the root of all evil."

"Money doesn't grow on trees."
"I'm not made of money."
"It takes money to make money."
"All rich people are greedy and snobs."
"The rich get richer and the poor get poorer."

How often as kids did we hear the terms "filthy rich" or "dirt poor"?—which is interesting, because whether there is too much or too little money, it apparently is unclean.

Our financial blueprint, like many of our other attitudes, will affect us for the rest of our lives—unless we work to change it. Our financial blueprint—like a blueprint for the construction of a house—represents the final plans. The dimensions and the design are set. Once we ratify the building blueprint, we cannot change it much. While we might like a much bigger, more extravagant house, we are only going to get a house that complies with the blueprint. If we want the house to be bigger or better (like "pie") we must change the blueprint. Just as the building blueprint sets the limits for our home, our financial blueprint determines the boundaries of our financial success—or failure.

We all know someone who seems to have "the Midas Touch," as everything they come in contact with always seems to become lucrative. Do these people have a built-in "money magnet," or do they possibly have a positive financial blueprint? By the same token, how many people do we know that whatever they do it always seems to result in a financial disaster? Do they have a built-in "money deflector," or perhaps a negative financial blueprint?

We have all read about individuals who won millions in a lottery only to become flat broke a year or two or so later. We have also all heard of professional athletes who make multi-millions in salary but are destitute shortly after they retire from active playing. According to this theory, if your financial blueprint is set for not having money, you will not have any.

In psychology a concept known as **Cognitive Dissonance** suggests that people are comfortable when their thoughts and feelings are congruent with their behavior, and are uncomfortable when their thoughts and feelings are in conflict (dissonant) with their actions. For example, suppose you have a friend that you have known for some time and you enjoy spending time with him or her. One evening while having dinner your friend has a few drinks and begins to speak in a rather racist manner. You had no idea until then that your friend was, in fact, a bigot. You are now in a state of **cognitive dissonance**: You pride yourself on being racially and culturally sensitive and diverse in your beliefs and thus are not comfortable being with someone who speaks in terms of racial and cultural stereotypes. Seeing your friend under the current conditions is now uncomfortable. To escape the dissonance you would either have to change your own views on race or choose to no longer have contact with your "friend." (You might also decide to never be with your friend when drinking is involved, or never bring up the topic of race, or make some excuses for your friend. In any case, your mind-set about your "friend" has forever changed and that relationship will be different—if it continues to exist at all.) Again, your thoughts and beliefs must be consistent with your actions.

My previous book, *The Graduate Course You Never Had*, was written for mental health practitioners to help them learn to more effectively develop, manage, and market a private clinical practice. In that book I refer to a conversation I had with another psychologist about securing more cash-pay clients—as opposed to managed -care (insurance-pay) clients. Early in the course of the conversation that psychologist noted he was struggling with finding many cash-pay clients. Near the end of the conversation he jokingly said, "I'm not sure I would want to pay $125.00 to see myself."

I laughed with him, politely.

The truth is if that clinician does not truly believe he is worth $125.00 a session, he is not going to get that fee. He was in a state of cognitive dissonance:

His thoughts said he didn't deserve $125.00 per session but yet that was the cash fee he was charging. More importantly, for our discussion, this therapist's financial blueprint was obviously set much lower than the $125.00 per hour fee he was seeking.

Recently, in my practice I met with an eight-year-old boy whose mother cleaned houses and father did landscaping. This boy often watched and sometimes helped his parents **work**. As part of introducing myself to this boy, I began to explain what a psychologist is and what kind of "work" a psychologist does. Midway through my explanation of what a psychologist does, the boy interrupted me and said, "This isn't work. You're just sitting in a big chair, in a nice room, and talking."

To this youngster, "work" meant manual labor. To him what a psychologist does is not "work"—it's just having a casual, social conversation in a nicely-appointed room. With this **Truth** firmly implanted in this boy's mind, what is his likely financial future? Is it likely that this boy will pursue higher education? Is it likely this boy will ever conceive of earning a living with his mind or by way of entrepreneurship? No, not very likely. This boy is most likely destined to become an adult who makes his living with his back— just as his parents did.

Now, I am certainly not saying that working with your hands is a bad thing. Laborers, technicians, masons, plumbers, electricians and mechanics are most important and definitely needed. I believe most people would agree, though, that working with one's mind is generally more profitable and clearly easier on the body, especially as we age.

The bottom line is that most of us get what **We Believe** we deserve. If you believe that there is no way in hell you can become financially free, you are right! Just like that little boy who could not fathom my "work" could entail sitting in a den-like office, or that fellow clinician who did not think he was truly worth the fee he was charging, your financial blueprint will ultimately determine your financial success or failure.

In my book on marriage, *How Come I Love Him But Can't Live With Him?*, I point out that money is one of the "Big Three" issues that trouble most marriages. Having counseled hundreds of couples over the past three decades, there is no doubt that *money*, *sex*, and *in-laws* are areas with which nearly all couples struggle.

Money is such a major problem because it represents much more than something you spend. Money represents security and power.

When two individuals come together to form a relationship, they have to effectively blend their divergent backgrounds. Each partner, therefore, brings his or her respective "financial blueprint" into the relationship. If they cannot achieve a satisfactory compromise or blending of their "financial blueprints," they are likely headed for trouble.

When my younger son Chad was about 12 we were watching college football on TV together one Saturday in the den. During a commercial Chad said, "Dad, Brian (his friend) and his dad are going fishing tomorrow morning at Bartlett Lake and Brian asked if I could go with them. Can I go?"

I responded, "Sure, no problem." But I felt a bit badly that I wasn't asked to go, too.

A few minutes later Nan came in from the garage from shopping. During the next commercial Chad went into the kitchen and I overheard him ask her for ten dollars for some art project he was doing the following week at school. Nan listened to him and then went into her purse and handed him a ten dollar bill. Chad thanked her, pocketed the bill, and then rejoined me on the couch.

A moment or two later I turned to Chad and said, "Chad, you earlier asked me if it was OK for you to go fishing tomorrow with Brian but then you waited until Mom got home to ask her for ten dollars for art supplies. Why didn't you ask me for the ten dollars at the same time you asked me about going fishing with Brian?"

Chad pondered a moment and then said, "Dad, you're easier with activities but Mom is easier about money."

I stopped and thought about what he had said and smiled. He was absolutely right. If he had asked Nan about fishing, she would have asked a hundred questions:

"Is Brian's father safety-conscious?"

"Will you have a safety vest?"

"Will you bring your sun screen?"

"What about getting enough sleep, if you have to leave so early in the morning?"

"What about breakfast tomorrow morning?"

And on and on.

By the same token, if he had asked me for the money, I would have asked:

"What exactly is the money for?"

"Was every kid told to get money from their parents?"

"Shouldn't you contribute something toward this?"

Chad, like most kids, had his parents completely figured out. Among many things, he understood a major piece of his parents' respective "financial blueprints."

While I was in the process of writing this book I met with this husband and wife about their 15-year-old son who was under-achieving in school. After meeting with Mother and Father for a few sessions and having them read my book (*Coping With Your Adolescent*), I asked to meet with their son.

Father brought the son in for the teen's first session but when I first met with Father to get an update before I met with the boy, Father said that there likely would be only a few more sessions because he was about to lose his job and insurance. The roofing contractor he worked for had just announced they were closing down.

Father related he had been with this company since he was 16 years old. He started out working there as a "gofer" and worked his way up to superintendent. He oversaw the production and the installation of the roofing product. He was now 52. He knew the business inside and out.

Father nearly came to tears as he described how he felt about losing "the only job I ever had."

"I gave them the best years of my life," he said. "I thought I would retire with this company. I have never been on a job interview before. I can't believe I have to find another job at this stage of my life." He also noted that he felt especially badly for some of the employees who were already let go. He was trying to help them find new jobs, as well.

I asked Father if he could see the end coming or was it a complete surprise. He said, "No, I was not totally surprised. I could see what they were doing right and what they were doing wrong. I tried to talk to them (management) but they wouldn't listen."

I then said to Father, "Let me see if I got this right. You've been with this company 36 years; you know this business extremely well. You know what this company did well and why it went under. You know the employees better that anyone in the company."

Father said "yes" to all the above statements.

I continued:

"If all of this is true (which apparently is the case) then why are you looking for a **job**, to work for someone else, again? Why aren't you talking about taking over the business yourself— perhaps with a few of your hand-picked employees? You could consider a small business loan, if necessary, or perhaps do something cooperatively with a few of your well-chosen employees."

Father gave me a "deer-in-the-headlight" stare and said, "Wow! I never even thought of that! It's funny; one of my best employees just yesterday asked me to take over the business; I didn't pay it too much attention—I thought he was joking."

Father said he would discuss the notion with his wife.

Clearly, Father's mind-set—"financial blueprint"—is forever to be a "**worker-bee**"—to have a job and always work for someone else. The concept of being "**the boss**" and running his own business was completely foreign to him—even when the opportunity stared him right in the face.

By the very same token, most mental health practitioners, for whom my last book was written, see one and only one way to earn a dollar. As I like to say in my workshops, "You must be seated in a room, with someone else seated across from you, and you have to pray that their insurance is good."

When I discuss "Alternative Methods of Earning Income" in the concluding half-hour of my workshop to mental health providers, I often get the same "deer-in the headlight" expression in the audience as I did from the Father referred to above who never considered taking over the roofing contracting business. I have often wondered that if the overwhelming majority of psychologists, counselors, and therapists are financially "stuck" in their "ruts," how can they effectively help their clients/patients to become "unstuck?"

Don't Know What to Do

You may want to get out of your "rut" but you don't have any idea how to do it. For example, if you begin to investigate how to become financially independent, you will be bombarded with books, CD's, seminars, and programs which will tell you to do various things and/or think in various ways. How are you supposed to know what program to follow? Since you are confused and overwhelmed, you typically do nothing—and remain "stuck."

To make any substantive change you will need to have a plan. We have all heard the adage:

"The road to hell is paved with good intentions."

Similarly, I firmly believe that "The road to our dreams often is unmapped."

Your goal may be to become financially free, but if you do not have a plan and a specific guide, you may never get there. By the time you have finished this book, you will have that plan and roadmap.

Not Enough Time

Without a doubt, another huge reason people give for not achieving their goals and dreams is:

"I don't have enough time."

I have been hearing this rationale for over 30 years. As one frustrated patient recently put it, "I'm too busy just making a living to make my fortune."

The irony of this statement so struck me, I used it for the title of this book. (In fact, the titles for each of my other books also came from clients, as well.)

I cannot tell you how many times in my career I've listened to a patient argue that they give so many hours to their unsatisfying job they simply have no time to search for a better one. Similarly, I regularly hear patients lament that they are too exhausted from their unfulfilling job that they do not have the energy, in addition to the time, to exercise or pursue a rewarding hobby.

Once again we see another negative circle:

People continue to use their time for activities that do not enhance their lives. This leaves them little or no time or energy to pursue endeavors that would improve their lives. If we believe we do not have the time to do something, even if it is beneficial, we simply will not do it.

Thus, again, we are "stuck."

While writing this book I began seeing a 40-year-old busy, successful stockbroker with family issues. He missed his third session due to having a seizure. He spent a day in the hospital and saw several physicians. When I saw him for his next appointment, about three weeks later, he related that his doctors ordered that he lose 40 pounds, reduce his stress, and begin an exercise program. He said he was simply too busy and it would cost him too much money to set aside time for exercise. I told him, "If you continue doing what you're doing, you may well become the richest guy in the graveyard."

He replied, "No doctor ever put it quite that way."

Realizing, finally, he needed to re-order his priorities, he joined a gym that afternoon. Here again, someone was devoting all his time to "making a living" to the neglect of his health. Being "stuck" in this "rut" could well lead to an early grave.

Not Enough Money

Another very common reason people give for not pursuing their dreams is, "I don't have enough money." Taking a class, joining a gym, eating healthier or taking time off from work to pursue a lead can cost money. Frequently I hear clients rationalize that their available funds are essentially committed, so they see no way they could put more money into a life-expanding endeavor. Once more, being stuck keeps you stuck.

I Don't Believe I Can Do it—or Deserve It

If no one in your family has ever attained personal or financial success, what makes you think you can? Many of us have witnessed considerable failure in our family, as we watched, for example, our parents struggle to "make ends meet." Given this negative **model**, which comprises, in large part, our **financial blueprint**, many of us have personally experienced failure in our quest for financial and personal success. Over time we reconcile ourselves to our "stuck" position.

To put it more succinctly, if you have witnessed failure in your models and experienced failure yourself, you are not likely to believe that you can be successful. We become "stuck" because we come to believe that we are destined to struggle—so why even try.

Women Returning to Work

Many women today are attempting to re-enter the work world after having their babies and raising their children full-time until the children are old enough to be in school all day. I have seen many such individuals in my practice. Many of these women were bright, educated, assertive individuals before they left the work place. However, several years later, after marrying, changing diapers, and reading bed-time stories, many of these women lose that creative, aggressive, entrepreneurial spirit they once had. Although they may desire to return to work, they now feel threatened and intimidated by that notion. They may also have to update their skills.

Unfortunately, our society does not seem to value motherhood (among other important things—like its elderly). Many once-successful women who chose to become full-time mothers for a time seem to buy into the negative view of parenthood and stop valuing themselves. This loss of self-worth makes it difficult to successfully transition to the world of work. Again, negative thinking prevents these individuals from reaching their personal and financial objectives.

Important Points to Remember in Chapter One

1. You are "stuck in a rut" because you keep doing the same things despite wanting a different result. If you want something different, you will have to act differently.

2. You remain stuck due to the allure of immediate gratification, fear of change, fear of failure, and even the fear of success.

3. Your financial blueprint, like the blueprint for a new building, sets the limits of your success.

4. Believing that you don't have enough time or enough money also keeps you "stuck."

5. You are "stuck" if you believe that since no one else in your family was successful, you, too, will have no chance to become successful.

6. Many mothers who want to return to the business world believe they no longer can be successful.

CHAPTER TWO

What Is Financial Freedom?

**"If you always do what you've always done,
you'll always get what you've always got."**

Three Categories of Financial Status

As I noted previously, I am not a financial expert. However, I have sat across from hundreds of clients for thousands of hours who speak of their struggles with money. I have seen money, or the lack of it, lead to divorce and depression.

The concept of financial freedom is a relative term. What is considered being financially free to Warren Buffet or Bill Gates, for example, is far different than what financial independence would be for the average man or woman.

I must also point out that for some individuals financial independence is not all that important to them. As long as they have sufficient funds to meet their basic needs, they are happy. They manage to enjoy life simply without chasing the mighty dollar. As the old saying goes, some people live to eat and some others eat to live. By the same token, some people live to work but others simply work to live. For these folks working provides for the basic necessities but most of what they enjoy in life is unrelated to their job.

As I see it, there are three different categories with regard to financial freedom:

Surviving,
Comfortable,
and Wealthy.

Surviving

As I described in CHAPTER ONE, most people today, unfortunately, are in the survival mode. They live paycheck to paycheck. Some months they have to choose to pay some bills over others. They have a large credit card balance and a limited or non-existent savings account. If they are laid off, get sick, become briefly disabled, or become faced with a sizable unexpected expense, they are immediately in a profound financial crisis.

Individuals in this position have limited funds to recreate, travel, or become educated. All available money is used to meet basic needs. Their lives in many ways are limited by lack of funds. They are frustrated.

Comfortable

People who are comfortable financially have managed to earn a level of income that exceeds their basic financial needs. Comfortable people are more able to travel, explore opportunities, and become educated. However, they are often not financially independent because they are completely dependent on their job or practice. If they lost their position or could not work, they, too, would be in a financial crisis.

For many individuals in this category they live by this unfortunate unwritten rule:

"As thy income rises, so shall thy expenses."

There are many folks who make a sizable income but their expenses are even more sizable. They may have even less liquid money than their employees.

Many persons in this category may look like they are successful:

They live in a big house, drive a nice new car, belong to an expensive golf club, and wear expensive clothes. Unfortunately, they are mortgaged to the hilt. They actually own very little, have minimum funds saved or invested, and may have a net worth comparable to many persons in the surviving category. In Texas folks like this are described as:

"Big hat; no cattle."

Thus, individuals in this situation continue to work because they have to.

Wealthy

Most people who are wealthy receive money not only from their jobs. It is likely most of their income is passive—from investments. For these folks, **"They don't work for money; their money works for them**." These individuals are truly financially free. If something happened to their job, it would be barely noticed due to the passive streams of income that would continue to flow to them. These individuals work because they choose to— not because they have to. To me, this is the true definition of financial freedom.

Some wealthy individuals, though, like many in the comfortable category, become overly-committed financially. Again, as noted previously, as their income continued to rise, so did their expenses. If they experience a significant downturn in their investments or the economy falls, they could quickly move out of the wealthy classification.

According to Drs. Stanley and Danko, authors of *The Millionaire Next Door*, if poor people fall into some money, they pay off bills and save any remainder at 1% interest. If middle class folks have money, they buy liabilities—cars, country club memberships, and bigger houses. If wealthy people get any additional funds, they invest it. In this manner poor people financially remain where they are; middle class individuals decline financially, and wealthy folks get richer. The "rich do get richer," but it is not due to fate; it is largely due to the poor choices non-rich people make and the smart choices wealthy people make.

The Path to Financial Freedom

I have had many clients tell me they will never be able to become financially independent because they will never have the education or connections to obtain that kind of *job* to provide the opportunity to become financially free. It may be true that you probably will not be able to go to medical school, law school, or graduate school when you are in your 40's or 50's (although it might not be entirely impossible).

A professional job, though, in most cases, is NOT the way to financial freedom. The path may be through **Entrepreneurship**.

My buddy Jeff likes to use this example to illustrate the important difference between a **job** and a **business**: Let's consider three young men who are about to start their careers.

Tom looks for a job;

Dick starts his own practice;

and Harry begins a business.

Tom secures an IT job that pays $50,000.00 per year.

Dick begins his accounting practice (it could be a counseling, legal, or a medical practice, for our discussion), becomes self-employed, and begins billing $75.00 per hour.

Harry starts to build his multilevel marketing business.

Where are these three individuals financially by the end of year one?

Tom has worked very hard and has made $50,000.00, per his salary.

Dick has also worked very hard setting up his practice and has spent considerable money on rent, staff, and material, and has a first year net earning of $25,000.00.

Harry, too, has worked hard building his downline. He has had relatively few costs to conduct his business, so at the end of the first year he has earned about $25,000.00, as well.

At the end of year two Tom has continued to work hard in his job, has received a nice raise, and earned $65,000.00 for that year; he feels he is doing well.

Dick's hard work is also paying off, as his practice has begun to grow and he earns $100,000.00 in year two.

Harry has also put in the necessary time and effort and he earns $75,000.00 for year two.

By the end of year three Tom is still working very hard at his **job** so he receives another decent raise and earns $85,000.00 his third year.

Dick continues to put in long hours in his practice and earns $150,000.00 for year three; he feels he is professionally on his way.

Harry has developed a long, solid downline of associates, such that several of his top associates are essentially doing all the training for him, so he is not working too hard anymore. Nevertheless, he earned $250,000 his third year in business. He is now thinking about starting a second business.

Tom must work hard to keep his job and his nice yearly raises.

Dick will also have to continue to toil long hours at his practice. Although his income is not constrained by a set paycheck, his income is limited by the number of hours he can possibly work in a week.

Harry may not be the most educated but may well be the richest of the three men. He has taken advantage of "leverage," which is having others doing the work for him, so he does not have to work so hard. He has also used the concepts of **duplicability** and **passive income**. Duplicability means once you have begun a successful business in one place you can start (duplicate) another successful business someplace else. Passive income means that you earn money without having to expend any additional time, effort, or money for it. Harry's income, therefore, has no ceiling. Starting a successful business—becoming an **entrepreneur**—therefore, is one of the quickest and perhaps easiest ways toward obtaining financial freedom.

I am not saying that you cannot become financially free by having a **job**. I should note that if Tom can save money while he continues to earn a decent income, he can use some of his savings to invest in income-producing (passive income) and/or income-growth (stocks, for example) opportunities. Also, if Tom continues to do well in the company, he could get promoted to vice-president of sales, for example, and some day even become CEO. Of course, at that point he is well on his way toward financial independence.

Like Tom, Dick can (and should) also invest in income-producing opportunities. While his income is limited by the number of hours he can work, he can multiply his efforts by hiring additional people to do more work and thereby benefit from their productivity. Finally, Dick and Harry can avail themselves of tax advantages far more readily than can Tom, where his taxes are withdrawn from his paycheck before he even receives it.

With the advent of the Internet there is no better time than the present to develop a business. A successful Internet business has no income limits. There are no salary boundaries and the income is not determined by the number of hours that can be worked. The Internet is open 24/7/365.

I have read reports of a successful Internet business being run by an adolescent. When you purchase something over the net, for example, you have no idea who is processing your order.

Example: Roy and his Truck

Last year, Roy, a middle-aged man, came into my office. He complained that his life was "blah." Roy was a warehouse manager and had no advancement opportunities in his position. He was bored with his job, there were no new challenges, but he could not afford to leave it. The "bloom was off the rose" with his 23-year marriage, as well. Finally, his two adolescent children were also providing him little joy.

After I obtained his history, I asked Roy, "What in your life do you find at least a bit exciting or enjoyable?"

Roy immediately answered, "My favorite thing to do is to work on my lifted truck." As we discussed his hobby of working on his truck, Roy noted that the after-market parts for his truck were extremely expensive. In fact, the parts were so costly, Roy's wife often would become upset with him because he spent too much money on his truck—which, of course, didn't help the marriage much. I suggested that Roy look into those truck parts and their cost.

At our next session, two weeks later, Roy said he carefully examined his two favorite catalogues for truck parts and noted that in both cases the parts were manufactured by an outfit in Pennsylvania. He decided to call that company and spoke with the Director of Marketing. It turned out that the Director told Roy that they were always looking for additional distributors to sell their products.

The Director told Roy he would send Roy a catalogue with the wholesale prices the manufacturer required. If Roy wanted to start his own distributorship, he would need to develop his own website, download the manufacturer's catalog, and then set his own prices. When Roy received an order he would email the order to the manufacturer, pay the wholesale price with his credit card, and the manufacturer would drop-ship the order directly to the customer. Roy would pocket the difference between the manufacturer's wholesale cost and Roy's retail price.

Roy noted that the catalogues he was previously using to purchase his parts were charging a mark-up of 200%. He thought he could develop a decent business with a margin of 100%. With a friend Roy developed a nice website. He also introduced several specials and incentives for customers to buy more and refer new customers.

A few months after Roy started his business he was getting a few orders every other day. He was excited about his new business, enjoyed the additional money, and especially liked being able to purchase his own truck parts wholesale.

The last time I saw Roy, about ten months into his new business, he was getting nearly a complete computer screen full of orders daily. He couldn't wait to come home from work—his **job**—and process all his orders each day—from his **business**. He was making two times more money in his **side business** than in his warehouse management **job**. He planned to continue to grow his business. His attitude on life had considerably brightened, his relationship with his wife also had improved, and even things with his kids got better, as well.

The Internet, as seen above with Roy, offers many, many distributorship types of opportunities. Direct sales are also possible. Finally, other great opportunities exist, such as in multi-level marketing companies. The point, of course, is that you don't need a Ph.D., MD, or JD to become financially free; you may only need a computer.

Important Points to Remember in Chapter Two

1. The three basic categories of financial status are: Surviving, Comfortable, and Wealthy.

2. Financial independence means having streams of passive income and working because you choose to; not because you have to.

3. You must always be careful to not allow expenses to keep pace with income.

4. The "rich get richer and the poor get poorer" largely because of the poor financial decisions poor people make and the smarter choices rich people make.

5. It is important to understand the differences between having a **job**, being **self-employed**, and owning a **business**.

6. The Internet provides more opportunities for an individual to become an **entrepreneur** and financially successful than ever before.

CHAPTER THREE

The Four Forces on Mankind

**"You are exactly where you
are supposed to be."**

What are the forces or influences that make us who we are?

How did we get to where we are today?

What factors led us to this position in our life?

These are important questions.

According to the science of **psychology**, the forces that essentially determine who and what we are and become are:

Our genes and our physiology;

our environment;

our conscious thoughts;

and our unconscious thoughts.

These factors—individually and in combination—ultimately determine our destiny.

For example:

Do you think that the sperm cell that fertilized the egg that became you, which carried either an X or Y chromosome and thus made you a male or a female, was significant in your development?

I believe so.

Do you think that being raised in a loving, nurturing home where education was valued, instead of being reared in an abusive, neglectful situation where education was ignored, may have played an important role in your overall functioning?

Yes, of course.

Do you think that considering positive, encouraging thoughts generally throughout your life instead of regularly contemplating negative, demeaning thoughts, could play a major role in who and what you become?

I think yes.

Finally, do you think having come to unconsciously believe certain **Truths** about yourself which are adaptive and productive instead of developing subconscious beliefs about yourself that are maladaptive and non-productive, may have affected your destiny?

I say absolutely.

Ever since I was an undergraduate psychology student I have found it fascinating that the four forces which shape mankind equate to the four basic schools of psychology. These schools are (in the order discussed above):

The Biological School,

The Behavioral School,

The Cognitive School,

and the Analytic (Freudian) School.

In the following chapters we will look more carefully at each school of thought. In particular, we will study what each school says about what is mental health, what is mental illness (being "stuck"), and what is treatment (getting "unstuck"). Perhaps even more importantly, we will look at what each school has to say with respect to achieving your life goals.

Let me also point out that most mental health providers subscribe to and practice according one of these schools. I believe the perspective of choice best fits the personality of the therapist.

The Biological School of Psychology

The biological model has been around the longest—for thousands of years. In the days of ancient Rome, Socrates classified men into several different personality types of which, it was presumed, they were born into.

The biological view purports that how an individual functions is largely dependent on his or her biology—his or her genetics and his or her physiology. We are born with certain features— male/female, white/dark skin, dark/light hair, brown/blue eyes, tall/short, intelligent/challenged, healthy/ill, and so forth. We are also born with certain proclivities or predispositions—temperament, other personality traits, addictions, tendency to be thin, and so on.

Obviously, the Biological model is the view of the physician—and, in the case of mental issues, the psychiatrist. To the psychiatrist mental health is essentially dependent upon biology. Individuals with mental health problems, then, for the most part, have an issue with their genes and/or physiology—a **chemical imbalance**. According to psychiatry, the primary treatment of most mental health concerns is medication to correct or improve that chemical imbalance. It is well understood, today, that many serious mental disorders, such as schizophrenia, bipolar disorder, obsessive compulsive disorder, depression, anxiety, autism, and even addictions, are genetically-based.

The Distinction between a Psychiatrist and a Psychologist

First, let me clarify the distinction between a psychologist and a psychiatrist. Many people do not understand the difference, including some folks who should know better, like journalists. It is unfortunate that the terms psychiatrist and psychologist are so long and difficult to say yet are so similar—just one syllable apart. For example, I recently read an article in the newspaper that some individual was court-ordered for a psychiatric testing. Psychiatrists don't do testing; psychologists do.

Psychiatrists, like psychologists, get their undergraduate degree usually in psychology or often in a natural science. Psychiatrists then go on to medical school. They are physicians. They have an MD after their name—which stands for medical doctor. After their four years of medical school they do a one-year internship and then a two-year residency in psychiatry. (If they specialize in child psychiatry, for example, they may need an additional two- or three-year residency.) Psychiatrists work in hospitals, clinics, in research, at universities, mental health centers, and in private practice.

Since psychiatrists are trained as physicians, they operate from a "Medical Model"—a biological perspective on health. Hence, psychiatrists are primarily representatives of the Biological school of thought. They understand and are concerned with the anatomy and physiology of the brain. The specialty of the psychiatrist is psychopharmacology—the understanding of brain chemistry and how certain medications (psychotropics) affect the brain and can improve mental health functioning.

Since psychiatrists believe mental illness is due to a "chemical imbalance," the primary intervention, then, is the prescription pad—"medication for the mind." Antidepressants and tranquilizers are, by far, the most common medications psychiatrists prescribe.

Today, psychiatrists primarily work in the area of psychopharmacology. In contrast to a generation or so ago, psychiatrists do relatively little psychotherapy. Up until about the 1980's training for most psychiatrists included training in psychoanalysis (Freudian psychotherapy, but more on that in the next chapter). Presently, training in psychotherapy for psychiatrists is relatively de-emphasized.

Psychologists, like psychiatrists, earn an undergraduate Bachelor's degree, often in psychology. Next, in graduate school—not medical school—psychologists earn a Masters degree and then a Doctoral degree—Ph.D. (Doctor of Philosophy) or Psy.D. (Doctor of Psychology). Psychologists then do a one to two-year internship. Like psychiatrists, psychologists work in hospitals, clinics, in research, at universities, mental health centers, schools, and private practice. Psychologists also specialize in clinical, organizational, neuropsychological, child, school, and forensic (legal) areas.

Psychologists are trained, to some degree, in the anatomy of the brain but receive little instruction in the pharmacology of the brain. Generally, psychologists do not adhere to the Medical Model and do not endorse the notion that mental health is essentially a function of one's genes and physiology. Psychologists believe that your mental health is more a function of your childhood experiences, education, how you think, and/or how you behave. Therefore, not too many psychologists are proponents of the Biological school.

Psychologists, since they are not physicians, cannot prescribe (with a few exceptions—but more of that in a minute). Psychologists work primarily by psychotherapy—"talk therapy" and education. Psychologists and psychiatrists often work hand-in-hand. There are psychiatrists in both of my offices in which I work.

The distinction between psychologists and psychiatrists has become more blurred over time. At the time of this writing, in the states of Louisiana and New Mexico, psychologists, with the proper training and internship, can prescribe psychotropic medication. In addition, psychologists, again with the proper training and internship, can prescribe psychotropic medication anywhere in the U.S. military. It should also be pointed out that approximately 80 percent of psychotropic medication is prescribed by general and family physicians, not psychiatrists. Moreover, in most states psychiatric nurse practitioners (NP's—nurses with a Masters degree) can also prescribe psychotropic medication. Finally, to further add to the confusion, other non-MD's, like dentists and physician assistants, under certain conditions, can also prescribe psychotropics.

Psychologists, too, do not stand alone. Therapists, counselors, psychotherapists and social workers, all typically with a Masters degree, also do work similar to that of psychologists. Thus, the number and types of professions in the field of mental health is quite varied. It is not surprising, then, that many people get confused.

So why is it important to understand the distinction between the psychiatrist and the psychologist? It is important because if you understand the difference in training and mind-set between the two professions, you will become a wiser consumer of mental health benefits.

I have had numerous cases in which clients come to my office for their first appointment and share with me that they were primarily concerned with managing their child's behavior, improving communication with their spouse, or needed tips on finding a better job. They noted they previously saw a psychiatrist and were disappointed with the results: They were offered a prescription for medication but were provided little in the way of relevant, useful advice.

I point out to those clients that they were "shopping in the wrong place. You don't look for a prom dress (or suit) in a hardware store." A hardware store, though, sells very useful things and dispenses very handy information—but not about what to wear for the prom. Generally speaking, I argue if you are concerned with a relationship issue, you are probably better off seeing a psychologist (or therapist) rather than consult a psychiatrist.

On the other hand, many individuals have come to see me for the first session and they are deeply depressed, extremely anxious, have uncontrolled bipolar disorder, have severe obsessive compulsive disorder (OCD), or are delusional. These individuals, I submit, first need psychiatric treatment—medication—before they could ever begin to benefit from treatment with a psychologist or a therapist.

Over the years I have had numerous cases where clearly understanding mental health issues, the various schools of thought, and the difference between a psychiatrist and a psychologist were crucial:

Last year I saw a middle-aged couple for marital therapy. They had been married over 25 years but were very unhappy. The wife loudly complained that her husband was "controlling, stubborn, and uncooperative." The husband noted that his wife was "argumentative, cold, and unaffectionate." They indicated that they had been to two marital counselors previously, with little results. If this episode of treatment with me was unsuccessful, they would probably consider divorce.

Upon conducting the initial intake it became evident to me that the husband had obsessive compulsive disorder (OCD). I recommended that before we have any additional marital sessions the husband should first see a psychiatrist and tell that psychiatrist that Dr. Waldman said that the husband likely had OCD.

I saw the couple eight weeks later. Husband had followed through on my recommendation. He saw a psychiatrist and was placed on an appropriate medication. The wife said that at the outset of our second session she already saw a huge positive change in her husband and for once was hopeful for the future of their marriage. I saw them for an additional six or seven times and their marriage improved significantly.

In this case the husband and wife failed to recognize the husband's specific mental health condition and where to go to get appropriate help. Also, two previous mental health professionals failed to identify the husband's condition or, perhaps, did recognize his condition but were unaware that medication could manage it. Nevertheless, here was a clear case where the value of psychiatry was initially unrecognized but ultimately was very helpful.

On the other hand, I am reminded of a case I had several years ago: A middle-aged woman was referred to me by her family practitioner. Sarah had numerous somatic complaints—including an ulcer, acid reflux, irritable bowel, near-continuous indigestion, nausea, diarrhea, frequent headaches, chest pain, to name just a few. She was on 15 different medications, prescribed by her family doctor, gastroenterologist, cardiologist, and neurologist. Some of those medications were also psychotropics. I recall she brought her medications to show me in a large plastic box, which was similar to a fishing tackle box, to keep her pills organized.

Being somewhat naïve, Sarah expressed confusion as to what a psychologist was and what one did. When I began to explain to her the role and function of a psychologist, she said, "I don't get it. My problem is in my stomach; not in my head." After some discussion we continued with the intake.

Sarah noted that she had been married over 30 years. When I asked her to describe the marriage she began to weep, but then said, "What does this have to do with my stomach?" Long story short, Sarah related that every Friday evening Herb, her husband, comes home from his work at the machine shop, eats dinner, showers, dresses, and goes out—alone—to the nearby tavern. He begins drinking heavily with his friends. As the bar closes, Herb leaves with a female "friend" and returns home. Herb and his "friend" spend the night in the master bedroom while Sarah sleeps in the guest room. Sarah makes breakfast for all that next Saturday morning.

I asked Sarah, "For how long has this been going on?"

She replied, "Years."

I then asked, "So how do you feel about this?"

To which she answered, crying, "How do you think I feel about it? I hate it!"

I next asked, "Have you shared your feelings with Herb about this?"

Sarah said, "Yes, many times, but he said he works hard and he deserves this."

At this point I told her, "Sarah, you might just be right. You may not, in fact, primarily need a psychologist. You probably need a good divorce attorney."

I saw Sarah for the next 12 to 14 months, off and on. She did see an attorney. Herb was asked to leave the home. He said he would stop his Friday night philandering but Sarah indicated she was not interested in his promises. She went back to work. She lost 30 pounds. She divorced Herb. She made some girlfriends and re-connected with her family.

When I last saw Sarah she was happy. She reported never feeling better—physically and emotionally. She was busy. She had met a nice gentleman in church. She was taking only three pills daily—a high blood pressure medication, a hormone, and a cholesterol pill.

In this case the Medical Model failed Sarah. Each physician she was seeing was looking at her through his own "periscope."

Each specific ailment allegedly needed a pill, but throwing a pill at each problem was not the solution. Sarah's problem was not primarily **medical,** it was primarily **psychological**; her stress was basically causing most of her medical issues. Unfortunately, no one was looking at Sarah as a "whole" person and asking the right questions. As a trained psychologist, I am inclined to look at the "whole" person. As the saying goes, "The whole is often greater than the sum of its parts."

Nature/Nurture

Biological markers are set and are not going to change much. We can do little or nothing about our gender (my apologies to transsexuals) height, eye color, or having certain genetic diseases.

On the other hand, some genetic predispositions may be related, in part, to the environment in which that individual lives. For example, if everyone in one's family is an alcoholic, presumably this individual is also genetically predisposed to become an alcoholic, as well. If this individual began to "experiment" with drugs and alcohol, as many young persons do, they likely would soon become an addict. However, if this person never abuses alcohol, or any other mind- or mood-altering drug, they will never become an alcoholic or drug addict. Thus, in some cases, the environment or one's mind-set (which, individually or in combination, influenced the individual to never drink) may play a significant role in determining if a particular genetic disposition is realized or not.

In psychology a common debate is over the "**nature/nurture**" issue. The issue is what factors are more powerful in shaping the person—their genetics (**Nature**) or how they were raised (**Nurture**). This topic has been discussed for decades and still is being investigated—particularly in twin studies where the subjects were raised apart. The answer is still not entirely in, but more and more the power of our genes is becoming recognized—but the effect of the environment cannot be ignored.

Being "Stuck"

With respect to becoming "stuck" it may be that we may not be "the brightest bulb in the pack," we and our entire family are overweight and out of shape, we may drink or drug too much, aspects of our personality are negative, we know nothing of building a secure financial future, and no one else in our family has ever done so.

So what is it, then, we should do?

We could say or think, "Well, I was born this way; there's nothing I can do about it; everybody in my family has the same problem, so why should I try to be different? I might as well just give up and do nothing—and let it be."

And this is exactly what most people do—and that is why they are "stuck" and "stay stuck." If everyone in your family, for example, is obese, does that mean you have to be obese, too? No, not necessarily. If "fat genes" run through your family it could very well mean that you have the predisposition to gain weight fairly readily. However, even with your genetic constitution, it is still up to you to decide what foods and in what proportions you consume them. If you choose to eat lots of sugary, starchy, fatty foods on a regular basis, especially with your genes, you will become obese. On the other hand, if you recognize your propensity to gain weight and choose instead to consume reasonable portions of nutritious, low-fat, healthy foods, you will likely become well-proportioned despite your genetics—just like the person from the alcoholic family who decided never to take a drink.

Have you ever noted what many overweight people have in their grocery shopping carts? I have. If you look, you will see things like soda, candy, snacks, beer, homogenized milk, ice cream, fatty meats, plus probably other "anti-slim" products. What you generally do <u>not</u> see, for example, in their carts is fruits, vegetables, low-fat yogurt, or skim milk.

Now, do overweight people become so because they were born that way? This would be the Biological (or Nature) reason. On the other hand, do people become overweight because of developing bad habits—poor eating and lack of exercise—which is the Nurture explanation? I believe the answer is, as usual, more complicated. I contend that our biology sets certain potentials, limitations, and proclivities for us, but it is our environment and our behavior which determine whether our potentials are met, limitations are exceeded, or our dispositions are fully manifested.

If someone is born with "fat genes," as an overweight adult they may give up in their "battle of the bulge." The more overweight you are, the more difficult it is to exercise.

As the law of physics states:

"A body that is in motion tends to stay in motion; but a body that is at rest tends to stay at rest." (This phrase refers to heavenly bodies—not human bodies—but the analogy fits.)

Recently, a client of mine who decided to get back to the gym said, "Just about everybody in the place (the gym) looks like they didn't need to be there." Funny, how that works.

I do most of the grocery shopping, as healthy eating, I believe, begins at the grocery store. Recently, while grocery shopping I witnessed a young boy, presumably less than two, behaving irritably in his seat in the grocery cart. I observed this young mother take an open bottle of orange, sugared soda, pour it into a bottle, and give it to the child. The little boy immediately began to suck the bottle vigorously and quickly became quiet. Later, I saw the child asleep in his seat, probably from the effects of the sugar. Now, was this poor child born to be fat or was he becoming trained to become so—and possibly diabetic, as well? By the same token, are some of us born to be poor or are we conditioned to become so?

As was noted earlier in this section, genetic predispositions can be substantially affected by environmental influences. For example, consider diabetes and bipolar disorder—two genetically-caused illnesses, one medical and the other mental. Both diseases are serious and potentially lethal if left untreated. Untreated diabetes can lead to heart problems, blindness and amputations. Bipolar disorder, untreated, can lead to crazy behavior, violence, divorce, drug use, broken relationships, jail, and even suicide.

It is well documented that if both syndromes are treated with consistent appropriate medication, proper diet, regular exercise, good sleep patterns, counseling, and refraining from excessive drugs or alcohol, the impact of these diseases on one's life will be minimal. There are many individuals with one of these disorders—sometimes with both disorders—who, with proper care, lead active, interesting, successful lives.

From the Biological perspective, why we get stuck is simple— we were born that way. How to get unstuck is much harder—we have to push ourselves to rise to the highest levels that our genetic potential will allow. For all we know we may even be able to push past our genetic "potentials."

How high is that potential? It is hard to tell. Few of us ever get there. We often marvel at obviously handicapped persons who have clearly pushed themselves to the very limits of their basic genetic potential—and even beyond, if that's possible. Just the other night I saw a TV special about a young woman who was born without legs who became a top-notch gymnast. If they can do it, why can't we—especially if we were not obviously handicapped in the first place?

Being born with certain (negative) attributes and predispositions is something most of us have to endure. We can allow the biological processes to completely rule us—and we will quickly become "stuck" in our "ruts." For many of us, it was not that we did anything wrong, we just simply gave into our natural impulses. We can **choose** to attempt to influence our biological forces as best we can. We can act right, think right, eat right, sleep right, get the proper care, and educate ourselves.

What to Do

So what are some of the things we can do to begin to strive to reach (even exceed?) our genetic potential?

Get a thorough physical exam and follow the physician's recommendations.

See a nutritionist and get on a proper eating plan.

Join a gym and get into a regular exercise program.

Schedule an appointment with a personal counselor to address your personal and/or relationship issues.

Schedule an appointment with you and your partner or child with a marital and/or family therapist.

Schedule an appointment with a financial counselor.

Attend a self-help group; for example: AA (Alcoholics Anonymous), NA (Narcotics A.), GA (Gamblers A.), or OEA (Overeaters A.).

Attend a support group—CODA, Alanon, CHADD (for parents of children with attention deficit disorder), a bipolar group, a diabetic group, whatever group might be appropriate for you.

Read a book related to a particular topic or area that you would like to improve.

Begin to read books on financial wellness. (To begin with, peruse this book's bibliography.)

Attend a seminar or workshop on marriage, parenting, and maybe even about investing.

The bottom line, from the **Biological** view, is that we may not be able to change our genes (at least at the time of the printing of this book) but we can **choose** to **do** things to modify our genetic forces. "We may not be able to change the cards we are dealt, but we certainly can decide how to play them." Remember, in poker the winner of the pot is not always the player with the best cards.

Important Points to Remember in Chapter Three

1. The four schools of thought in psychology are the Biological, Analytic (Freudian), Cognitive, and Behavioral.

2. According to the Biological view, mental health is a function of our genes and physiology; mental illness is due to a chemical imbalance; and treatment is the administration of psychotropic medication to remedy that chemical imbalance.

3. The psychiatrist goes to medical school, has an MD, follows the medical model, and writes prescriptions for psychotropic medication. The psychologist attends graduate school, has a Ph.D. or Psy.D., adheres to a sociological/educational model, and provides treatment via talk therapy (psychotherapy). Most prescriptions for psychotropic medication are written by family doctors, not psychiatrists, and many non-MD's today can also write prescriptions. Psychologists, with the proper credentials, in New Mexico, Louisiana, and in the military, can prescribe. Counselors, therapists, and social workers also provide psycho-therapy. The mental health field for the average consumer of mental health services is rather confusing.

4. The classic Nature/Nurture issue concerns whether we are who we are due to Nature (biological) forces or Nurture (environmental) factors. As usual, the answer is complicated. Science has found that Nature forces are more influential than previously believed; but environmental influences cannot be ignored.

5. Almost regardless of our genetic coding, we can still choose to behave or think in certain ways.

6. There are numerous ways to optimize our genetic potential—medical treatment, improved nutrition, regular exercise, counseling, education, and support groups.

CHAPTER FOUR

The Analytic View

"The past is always present but it need not be repeated."

Freud and the Analytic School

Chronologically, the Analytic view comes next. Sigmund Freud promoted his innovative (at the time) theories in the late 1800's in Vienna, Austria. Though a physician, he gave relatively little attention to biological processes. Instead, he theorized a psychological structure of the mind, or "psyche." At birth we are born with an "**id**"—the portion of the mind that is basic, instinctual, and wants all its needs met instantly (instant gratification). In early childhood the "**ego**" begins to develop, which is the part of the psyche that tries to control and socialize the primitive impulses of the id. Finally, around pre-adolescence the "**super ego**" begins to form—which essentially is the moral part of the psyche, or the conscience.

Freud argued that the id, ego and superego interact and battle among themselves throughout the individual's lifetime. For example:

A young adult man sees an attractive female. The id might urge the man to run up to her and proposition her immediately. The ego might counter and suggest that such impulsive behavior is unacceptable and might get you slapped or put in jail; instead, strike up a conversation with the lady, ask her out, and then see what happens. Lastly, the super ego might remind the young man, "No sex until you are married!"

Freud also postulated a theory of "Psycho-Sexual Development," through which all individuals must successfully traverse to become a mentally healthy adult. The five stages, with their general age range, and the specific "crisis" to be resolved in each stage, are as follows:

Oral—0 to 2 years—weaning;

Anal—2 to 4 years—toilet training;

Phallic—3 to 6 years—masturbation;

Latency—pre-adolescence—no crisis; and

Genital—adolescence to early adult—adult sexuality.

According to Freud, one's mental health was a function of effectively going through the developmental stages, appropriately resolving the "crisis" of each stage, and, of course, having the id, and ego, interact as smoothly as possible. Mental illness in the adult, on the other hand, Freud defined as becoming hung up or "fixated" in one of the psychosexual stages in childhood. Thus, per Freud, the mental symptoms presented by the adult are essentially irrelevant, as they represent the "unconscious unresolved conflict" of the child.

Treatment, or "**psychoanalysis**," as named by Freud, consisted of 90-minute long sessions, two or preferably three times per week, for at least a year, in which the "patient" lies on a couch, facing away from the therapist, and "free associates" about his or her childhood, especially about their recollections of their interactions with their mother. The therapist, or psychoanalyst, is relatively passive during the sessions. Dreams are also of interest and are discussed because Freud believed that dreams came directly from the unconscious.

The goal of the treatment is "**catharsis**"—in which the patient finally comes to understand why they became fixated in a particular stage and how that fixation has affected them as an adult. The unconscious conflict finally becomes conscious. As a crude example, someone who is an alcoholic or overeats may come to recognize that he or she was weaned too early—and thus became fixated at the oral stage.

Freud also postulated that humans regularly use **Defense Mechanisms**, which are various techniques that stem from our unconscious which help us protect ourselves emotionally.

Repression, denial, rationalization, and projection were all popularized by Freud.

Freud's work today is not well-accepted. Surveys in the 1950's and 60's found that the vast majority of mental health professionals practiced in a Freudian-based manner at that time. Such surveys today, though, find that less then ten percent of mental health professionals use the Analytic approach in their practices.

Freud's theories are difficult to research and are quite impractical, as most clients don't have the time, patience, or money to see a therapist for 90 minutes, three times a week, for a year or more. Moreover, certainly no health insurance carrier would pay for such extended treatment. Additionally, his work has been criticized as overly sexualized, Victorian-era based, and even misogynistic.

My Simplification

While Freud's views may be somewhat out-dated and impractical, I do not believe that his work should be entirely discarded. At times, I have found some of Freud's theories to be useful. Perhaps it may be a bit of an over-simplification, and my apologies to true analysts, but I like to conceptualize much of Freud's work in terms of what the child first learned—and accepted to be **true**.

The child, unlike the adult, has no perspective. The child cannot have an experience and then compare and contrast that incident with all the life experiences he/she has previously had— as would an adult. What the child experiences early on in their life he or she accepts, unfiltered, uncensored, unedited—as the "**Truth**." The child has nothing with which to compare their experiences so the child, therefore, is all-accepting and completely naïve. The child's mind is like a "**blank slate**;" what is first written on it is essentially indelible. Freud basically called this the "**unconscious**," but I like to refer to it as the child's "first learning's" or "implicit learning"—the things we, as adults, "learned" as a child and simply accept today as valid and the **Truth**.

For example, studies have shown that many children, often by age ten, have prejudices against certain racial or ethnic groups, yet many of these children have had little or no experience with such people. Obviously, these children "learned" their biases from their parents, assumed their biases were valid, and, unfortunately, in most cases, will maintain them into adulthood—and probably will "teach" their children the same "Truths," as well.

Example

About two years ago I had an interesting case in which the Analytic view came in handy: Sandy was an attractive, intelligent woman, in her early thirties, who was married with two young daughters. She worked as an assistant manager at a large, busy bank and was slated to soon become a branch manager. She came to me because for the past year or so she had been having anxiety or panic attacks. According to Sandy, these attacks would come "out of the blue" for no apparent reason and would last about 90 seconds or so. They would occur generally two-three times a week—some weeks more or less. Often she would have to sit down and calm herself for a few minutes following a panic incident.

When I first interviewed Sandy she seemed emotionally stable. She reported that her marriage was solid, her girls, 5 and 8, were well-behaved and doing well, and she enjoyed her job, liked the people she worked with, and was excited about her impending promotion. Apparently, then, there was nothing in her daily life that would account for the panic—so current **environmental** reasons could presumably be ruled out.

Sandy also noted in the interview that to her knowledge no one in her immediate family ever had any problems with depression or anxiety. Sandy also denied using drugs or alcohol. Thus, it would appear that there was no **biological** explanation for her problem.

Since Sandy's panic could not be explained by her current environment or by biological factors, it was time to dig deeper—

and I put on my Analytic hat. When we began to discuss her childhood Sandy reported a relatively normal, happy experience, but she became visibly tense as she talked about her early years. Knowing that one out of three women today has experienced some form of sexual abuse, I asked her if she was ever the victim of sexual misconduct—and she broke down.

Sandy related that from the time she was about 8 until about 11 an older (by about three years) male cousin who lived nearby and frequently visited the house and had "played doctor" with her many times. Crying, Sandy said at first she liked the attention from her older attractive cousin (and sometimes it felt good) but she ended it when she came to recognize it was wrong. She never reported the abuse to anyone, including her husband.

When I asked Sandy what she "took away" from that abuse, she said, crying louder, "I can't believe I allowed it! I feel so dirty! I'm so ashamed!" I pointed out to Sandy that on the outside she presents as a happy, well-rounded person but inside she believes she is guilty, dirty, and unworthy. These beliefs (**Truths**) are clearly the cause of her panic. Moreover, it seemed to me, the reason her panic started within the past year was due to the fact that her oldest daughter was approaching the age at which Sandy's abuse began. Tearfully, Sandy agreed.

I noted to Sandy that she has been living as an adult according to a Truth she developed when she was 11 years old that she is a shameful, unworthy woman. She has tried mightily to make it appear she is OK, but her internal conflict is showing in her panic attacks. Clearly, it was time for Sandy to amend her belief. Sandy said she was uncertain if she could do that because she truly felt shameful—but I had a response.

I said to Sandy that according to her belief, if, god forbid, her daughter were to tell her that someone had touched her inappropriately, Sandy would have to tell her daughter it was her daughter's fault, that she was to blame, that she was bad, that she was dirty, and that she should be ashamed of herself—forever! Sandy gasped and said, "No! I would never say that! I would kill him! It's my greatest fear!"

In response, I said:

"So you were guilty and dirty but, again, god forbid, your daughter would be a victim." Finally, at that point Sandy came to see how illogical her long-held Truth was, because she, too, was also a victim.

I believe in the notion that new information is the basis for change. I recommended that Sandy immediately speak to her husband about her abuse—and continue to re-think her **Truth**.

I saw Sandy two weeks later. She had a great conversation with her husband and he was understanding, warm, and supportive. She had not had a panic episode since I last saw her. I never saw her again after our second session, presumably because there was no need. Freud was right in this case. The Truths we glean from our childhood may haunt us unless we properly deal with them.

The Effect of Abuse

When children are abused they believe that the treatment they received was deserved. The children cannot comprehend that their parent(s), or some other favored adult, might be flawed. In their young innocent eyes, familiar adults are seen as gods. As they live in an abusive home they assume they are bad and unworthy. Child abuse not only harms the child at the time it is administered. Abuse has an indelible negative impact on the child's sense of self-worth which adversely affects the child's emotional development for years to come.

Another Classic Example

Let's consider a hypothetical, but classic, and unfortunately common, life story from an Analytic perspective:

Susan was born into a lower middle-class family. Her Father was a blue collar worker who liked his beer. Her Mother was primarily a homemaker but worked part-time at the school as a playground and cafeteria aide. Susan also had a brother about two years younger.

Susan's childhood recollection of her Father was that he would come home from a long day of work at the auto shop, sit in his favorite lounge chair, watch TV, and have several beers before dinner. Father was emotionally unavailable to Susan. She remembered often trying to engage him but he frequently would dismiss her, saying he was too tired and would speak to her later—but later rarely came. After dinner Father would return to his favorite chair and have another beer or two, or three. Many evenings Susan would go to bed while Father was asleep in his chair.

On weekends Father usually did some work around the house, like cutting the grass—"man's work"—and then go somewhere with his friends. He often did not return until Susan was in bed. When her brother got older, Susan noted that Father would take him on weekends but rarely did he take Susan somewhere.

Susan's Mother was quiet, unassuming, and depressed. Susan's childhood recollection of her Mother was cleaning, cooking, cleaning, doing housework, shopping, and cleaning. Susan remembers her Mother rarely laughed and hardly ever smiled. Susan and her Mother did things together, especially on weekends, like grocery shopping, but most of the time she and her Mother cleaned the house together. Susan recalls her brother rarely, if ever, was asked to do any of the household chores. In fact, Susan frequently was asked to clean up after him.

Susan saw few, if any, signs of affection between her parents. She recalls her Father often yelling at her Mother. Sometimes his words bordered on being abusive. A few times a month during an argument Mother would go into the bedroom and slam the door. Susan would hear her Mother crying.

Money was always an issue, as there was little of it. Father earned a modest income and Mother earned very little in her part-time work. Father "managed" the money and often had to leave some bills unpaid at the end of the month. Mother used to hide money when she could. Mother and Father regularly fought over finances.

Susan did well in elementary school, earning A's and B's. She was considered to be fairly bright, quite shy, and rather quiet. She had two close girlfriends, who were much like her.

When Susan was 12 she had her first "boyfriend." He was not nice to her.

By the time Susan was 13, as she was about to enter high school, she had learned several **Truths**. It was not as if her Father or Mother sat down and talked with her regarding the "facts of life." Instead, being a bright girl she looked at life as she knew it and naturally came to several conclusions—or "**Truths**."

They were:

1) Women are second class citizens.
2) Men are powerful but necessarily evils.
3) Women must try hard to receive attention from and be accepted by men.
4) A woman's job is to be a housewife.
5) Money is a problem—as there is never enough. The man manages it and the woman sneaks it.
6) Finally, and most significantly, Susan came to believe she was not valued. Her self-worth was low.

Now given Susan's life, her conclusions—"Truths"—were not inappropriate. Any reasonable girl raised in her environment would have come to the same beliefs.

So how did these truths come to impact Susan? In high school Susan's grades began to decline. Since she believed she was not that smart (though she actually was) and certainly saw no reason to consider going to college, she reduced her academic effort. Besides, no one else in her family had ever gone to college so why would she think she could handle college. There was also no way she could afford it. Finally, she was going to be a housewife, anyhow.

As Susan became sexually mature she naturally became interested in boys and they became interested in her. Since she "knew" that she had to work hard at getting male attention and figured that they would not be interested just in her "sparkling personality," she quickly recognized that if she offered sex, male attention was plentiful—albeit fleeting. Susan's frequent sexual encounters, unfortunately, reminded her of the mistreatment by her first boyfriend, and led to more degradation of her self-esteem.

At age 18 Susan became pregnant and dropped out of school to raise her child—a daughter. (Susan had become drunk at a party and was uncertain of the father.). Her parents were mortified and frequently, when upset, lamented, "How could you do this to us?"

Susan, with her daughter, lived at home with her angry parents, but managed to obtain her GED when she was 20. She took a second shift cashier job at the local grocery store so she could work and her Mother could provide childcare.

At 25 Susan married John, one of the evening stockers at the grocery. He, too, was a high school dropout, as he always had problems with paying attention in class. John liked to party, had experimented with many different drugs, and very much liked his beer—as did his father. (Down deep, Susan wasn't in love with John but she liked his attention—and believed that she probably wouldn't do much better.) Susan was pregnant at their wedding.

At age 30 Susan enters a therapist's office. She is depressed, overweight, and overwhelmed. Her marriage is unsatisfying, her daughter is on an antidepressant and is struggling in school, and her five-year-old son was just diagnosed with attention deficit disorder. She laments to her therapist:

"How did all of this happen to me?"

In a nutshell, if you believe certain Truths (positive or negative) about yourself that you glean as a child, you will behave according to these beliefs, and then you will have real life experiences (positive or negative) which substantiate those beliefs. This circle of beliefs, behaviors, and experiences ex-plains why many people function as adults according to the path that was carved for them as children. It also helps to explain why they remain "stuck in their rut."

Common Faulty Beliefs/Truths

With respect to the purpose of this book, what are some the "**Truths**" that many people have—that serve to keep them stuck?

"Only the rich get richer."

"It takes money to make money."

"Money is the root of all evil."

"The banks and the stock market are controlled by Jews."

"Investing is only for the rich."

"Wealthy people are all snobs and are selfish."

"It takes too much time to work out regularly."

"Most people who work out regularly are vain."

"I am not a worthy, valued person."

"Since my parent(s) mistreated me, how can I expect—or deserve—others to treat me respectfully?"

"I was spanked by my parents and I turned out okay."

"Everyone in my family has been divorced; what's the big deal?"

"You have to be crazy to see a mental health professional."

"I'm not going to a doctor for a checkup, it's expensive, and they will kill you."

What to Do

From the Analytic perspective, then, the "**Truths**" we initially learned as children and we blindly accept as the "gospel" as adults tend to keep us "stuck." What, then, can we do to get unstuck?

To get out of our "ruts" we first have to **acknowledge,** and second, **reassess,** some of our long-held beliefs. We may have to question some of our biases, prejudices, and knee-jerk adages, like "Only the rich get richer." Once we understand how we derived some of our "beliefs," we must as adults change our beliefs—or "change our mind." Remember, new information can lead to change.

We all have "changed our mind" about one thing or another at one time or another. If we know that we blindly, "unconsciously," accepted a belief as a child that was untrue and contributes to us remaining "stuck" in our "ruts," then why can't we change it?

We can and we should.

As adults we should strive to let go of negative, faulty, immobilizing beliefs which we formed as children and maintain throughout our adulthood. Frankly, many adults live out their entire life according to what was set for them early in their childhood. My definition of "**personal growth,**" then, is the ability to modify and step away from some of our childhood beliefs that serve to restrict us and keep us from growing, changing, and moving forward.

Select an area that you want to change for the better— financial growth, improve your physical conditioning, become a better parent or improve your relationship with your spouse— whatever. Then spend some time thinking about your immediate, reflexive views you hold about that topic and **write** them down. **Read** them aloud. **Analyze** them. Then, **question** them. Your beliefs may have been valid when you were a child, but does it make any sense to hold on to them as an adult? Lastly, **re-write** your beliefs about your chosen objective to reflect your updated, healthy, growing, *new* "**Truths**." Finally, you must *act* according to your new truth.

Let's take an example. Suppose you are an adult woman in a marriage that you decide should work better. Following the Analytic perspective, here are the steps to take:

Step 1: **Think** about your relationship and the implicit views you hold about it. For example, they might be:

"A marital relationship is not expected to be a happy one."

"I deserve to be treated indifferently and/or disrespectfully."

"A woman never has a say in how the money is spent."

Step 2: **Write** these **Truths** down and read and re-read them.

Step 3: **Analyze** these **Truths**. Come to understand why you came to believe them. (You probably want to consider your parents' marriage—or the lack of such.)

Step 4: **Question** these **Truths**. Are these Truths valid? Do I still need to keep believing them? Why should I live my life as an adult according to the perceptions of a child?

Step 5: **Re-write** your **Truths** and re-read them. They could be something like:

"A marriage can and should be a loving, warm, intimate relationship."

"I deserve to be treated in a caring, respectful manner."

"I should have equal say in how the household finances are managed."

Step 6: **Act** according to your new **Truths**. Remember, you will never be treated any better than you think you deserve. Speak lovingly to your partner, share your ideas, and request that both of you behave accordingly. Also remember, the best way to receive affection or respect from your partner is to first provide it to your partner. I call it "Give to Get." When some of that "old stuff" creeps back into interactions, you must gently but assertively challenge it—as you don't live that way any more. You may want to contact a personal and/or marital therapist to assist you in your quest to achieve one or more of your life's goals.

Through this process of **Writing** you Truth, **Analyzing** your Truth, **Questioning** your Truth, **Re-writing** your new Truth, and **Living** your **new** Truth, you will be taking a major step, from the Analytic perspective, toward personal growth, becoming "unstuck," and achieving your personal, life goals.

Important Points to Remember in Chapter Four

1. The Analytic view purports that mental health is based on the individual successfully passing through the five "psycho-sexual" stages of development (Oral, Anal, Phallic, Latency, and Genital) and having the components of the "psyche" (id, ego, and super ego) interact smoothly.

2. Mental illness, per the Analytic/Freudian perspective, is becoming "fixated" (hung up) in one of the developmental stages. This "unresolved conflict" in the child is manifested in subsequent psychological problems in the adult.

3. Mental health treatment, according to this school, takes the form of "psychoanalysis"—2-3 90-minute sessions per week in which the patient tries to bring the unresolved unconscious issues to the conscious level—thereby achieving "catharsis."

4. The "unconscious" may be understood in terms of the "Truths" we develop during our childhood. These "Truths" then guide us—good or bad—into our adulthood. Many adults continue to lead the life that was set for them before they were ten years old.

5. The steps to take to achieve our personal goals, according to the Analytic view, are: Consider an area you would like to improve. **Think** about your long-held beliefs (Truths) about that topic. **Write** those Truths down. **Analyze** them. **Question** them. **Re-write** your new, healthy Truth(s). Finally, **act** according to your new Truth.

CHAPTER FIVE

The Cognitive View

**"You cannot solve a problem with the same
kind of thinking that created it."**

Albert Einstein

History

Around 1900 in Germany, partly in response to Freud's work, a new form of psychology developed which became known as Gestalt psychology. "Gestalt" in German means "whole"— as in "greater than the sum of its parts." In a short time Gestalt psychology came to the U.S., where it was renamed Cognitive psychology. Cognitive psychology has since spun off Humanistic and Positive psychology.

Theory

Cognitive psychology is considered a "contemporary" theory, in that the focus is on the present, not the past, as in Analytic/Freudian psychology. Cognitive psychology is also a more positive view and less fatalistic, in contrast to Freud's work and the Biological school. Freud's view is considered fatalistic in that the unconscious, unresolved conflicts of the child are destined to plague the individual later in adulthood and in the Biological view our genetic influences are essentially unchangeable. Per the Cognitive view, on the other hand, people can readily change and grow.

In Cognitive psychology what is critical is what the individual is currently **Thinking**—not their genes, physiology, or their childhood experiences—hence, the term Cognitive. According to

Cognitive theory, what the person **thinks** determines how he or she **feels**. Then the individual **behaves** accordingly.

Most people use the terms "think" and "feel" as synonyms. They intersperse the terms "I think" and "I feel" in their conversations, intending to say the same thing. However, in Cognitive psychology the terms "think" and "feel" are different and distinct, but contiguous. First you think, then you feel, and ultimately you behave. The process is sequential and very quick, but also entirely conscious. "Cognition before emotion" is a Cognitive rule.

Proponents of the Cognitive model propose a three-stage model to explain much of human behavior: First the person receives some information (auditorily, visually, or kinesthetically), processes the input, then gives meaning to it—all of which is part of **cognition**. Second, the person determines how he or she **feels** about the input that has been received. Finally, in the third and last step, the individual **acts** according to the feeling he or she generated. The first step—cognition—is considered to be the most important—as cognition leads to a feeling which ultimately results in behavior.

An example of the Cognitive view in action is taking place right now as you, the reader, are perusing this material. As you read this prose you are continually sending visual cues, in the form of printed letters, to your brain. Your brain is instantly processing these little ink marks from the page into letters, then into words, and then into sentences. Almost in an instant—it seems almost miraculous—you, the reader, have read my information and have comprehended what I am trying to convey. This is stage one— **cognition**—the processing of the input.

Now that you have read and understand what I have written, you, the reader, will move to stage two, which is to determine a **feeling** about my words. Hopefully, after reading and digesting what I have written thus far, you, the reader, will generate a feeling something like this:

"I like what Larry has to say; it's interesting, innovative, and stimulating."

Now if that is the case—which, of course, is my hope—you, the reader, will **behave** by continuing to read my book, go about making positive changes in your life, and maybe will tell others to read the book as well. If, on the other hand, upon reading my material you, the reader, come to **feel**, for whatever reason, my information is unsuitable for you, you will likely behave by discontinue reading and perhaps telling others to not bother with the book.

In the process of cognition what you think is essentially what you tell yourself. It is not as if you are speaking aloud to yourself—as that would look weird and could get you in trouble. Thinking, then, is implicit "**self-talk**."

For decades I have had clients tell me that a feeling of depression, anxiety, or anger simply "comes over them." They don't understand how or why this happens. "It just does," they say. As a psychologist who often practices Cognitive psychology, I first have to help these clients recognize that their feelings do not evolve out of thin air. These emotions come from their own thoughts—their self-talk. If they are feeling depressed, anxious, or angry, they first had to contemplate such associated thoughts—and engage in negative self-talk.

Cognitive psychology proposes that our thoughts stem from our self-concept (or self-esteem or self-image)—our sense of **Self**. The **Self** is a collection of learned, completely **conscious** beliefs we hold about ourselves. (This is different from the unconscious Truths we derived from our childhood, of which we are unaware in our adulthood—per the Analytic school.) The **Self** is comprised of numerous beliefs we have about all aspects of our being. For example:

How smart/dumb we think we are.

How strong/weak we are.

How likeable/dislikeable we are.

How good/bad a student we are.

How good/bad a spouse or parent we are.

How good/bad a dancer we are.

We learn our particular beliefs through our experiences. In time our beliefs become like habits. We all develop behavioral habits—some good ones, like making the bed every morning or working out every Monday, Thursday, and Saturday—and some bad ones, like biting our fingernails or eating a dish of ice cream nightly before bed. We also develop good and bad **thinking** (self-talk) habits. Just like with behavioral habits, when in a particular situation (such as bedtime and we need ice cream) we tend to almost automatically think certain thoughts. For instance, for some people when they are confronted with a challenge of some sort they almost immediately begin to think they will surely overcome it; but other people instantly think they are likely to fail.

Let's consider the situation in which a young man, with a fragile self-concept (**Self**), is about to face a job interview. As he is sitting in the outer office waiting to be called upon, he thinks (tells himself):

"I hate these interviews. They make me so tense. I never do well in them. Do I really have a shot at this job or do they already have someone in mind and they are just going through the motions? I already have had four other interviews and haven't received a job offer. What chance do I have with this one?"

Clearly, with this kind of negative thinking operating in his mind this interviewee is likely to perform in a sub-optimal manner. This less-than-stellar performance, then, is likely to result in another failed job attempt. As this young man walks away from the building toward the parking lot, again without a job offer, he thinks (tells himself), "I knew it! Why did I waste my time?"

This young man's poor self-esteem led to negative thinking (I like to call it "**Stinkin Thinkin**"), which caused sub-par perform-ance, which resulted in another failure, which caused him to endorse his original negative belief. This self-defeating, negative, self-fulfilling cycle is an example of how people develop and maintain a critical, fragile **Self** and perpetuate their "stinkin thinkin."

My Son Josh

My older son Josh worked hard and did well in law school. As he approached graduation, he began to look for a job. Now if you graduate near the top of your law class many law firms looking for a new associate will come calling. Josh had a few initial interviews but received no job offers. I began to wonder what was going on.

One day while speaking by phone with my son he noted he had another interview coming up. He said he had heard good things about that firm and really hoped that the firm would make him an offer. There was something about the way Josh talked that caused me to say, "Josh, it kind of sounds to me like you are going into this interview with your hat in your hand."

He said, "Dad, what does that mean?"

I replied, "It is an old expression that implies you are being somewhat obsequious—like begging, almost, for the job. Law firms don't want to hire pansies; they want aggressive, talented tigers."

I said the following:

"Didn't you graduate at near the top of your class? Don't you work hard? Haven't you learned how to effectively manage your time? Aren't you intelligent? Aren't you willing to learn? Aren't you a quick learner? Aren't you loyal? Aren't you persistent? Aren't you an athlete with a strong drive to excel? Aren't you a good-looking young man?"

Josh answered yes to all these questions.

"If all of this is true," I said, "then wouldn't you be a major asset to any firm that hired you?"

Josh agreed he would.

I next said, "Then go into your next interview telling yourself that they would be foolish not to hire you!"

The next three interviews all led to offers. Josh's "please-hire-me" thinking was causing him to feel somewhat intimidated which behaviorally came across as being too passive—which impeded his job search. After several years of practicing business litigation law, Josh certainly has learned to become assertive.

When Josh was in high school he was an excellent runner—number two in the state in the 800—two laps around a quarter-mile track. During his junior year, I believe, I was driving Josh one very early Saturday morning to a regional meet in Casa Grande, mid-way between Phoenix and Tucson. As we were chatting in the car, Josh mentioned that some guy in Tucson had recently posted an 800 time that was about a half-second better than Josh's best time, thus far. Josh then said something like, "I guess I'll take second place today."

I looked in my rearview mirror and quickly pulled onto the shoulder of the interstate. I said, "Josh, if you are telling me you are already content with second place today without running the race and are essentially going to simply 'mail it in,' then I might as well turn around at the next exit and go home." I continued, "When you and that guy are neck and neck with about 100 meters to go and your lungs feel like they are going to burst and you are thinking that second place is good enough, what are you going to do?"

Josh replied, "Come in second, I guess."

I answered, "You are exactly correct! Now, when that guy expects you to back off but you don't, the pressure is on him."

Josh won his event by five meters.

Bottom line:

"If you believe you will come in second, you will never be first."

Cognitive psychologists often talk about the **Law of Attraction**. This refers to the notion that what we think about expands. If we think good things and speak to ourselves in a positive manner, then good things will happen. However, by the very same token, if we think bad thoughts and speak to ourselves in a negative manner, then bad things will occur.

Theory of Mental Health

From the Cognitive view, then, good mental health occurs when the individual develops a positive **Self** system and generally thinks and speaks to himself or herself in a self-encouraging, self-supportive manner.

Theory of Mental Illness

Cognitively speaking, mental illness occurs when the individual frequently engages in negative, critical, and non-supportive thinking. As noted above, a self-defeating, self-fulfilling pattern develops which consists of negative thinking ("Stinkin Thinkin"), which leads to poor performance, which results in failure, which then is used to confirm the original pejorative thinking. This **Self-trap** can lead to depression, anxiety, and a sense of helplessness; it prevents people from moving forward and keeps them "**stuck**."

Theory of Treatment

Mental health treatment, from the Cognitive view, consists of having the therapist help the client understand the process that how one **thinks** leads directly to how one **feels**, which ultimately results in how one **behaves**. Next, the therapist assists the client to think (and speak to himself or herself) in a more realistic, present, positive, and supportive manner—and avoid the **Self**-trap.

"Change the thinking and you change the feeling" and, ultimately, you "change the behavior"—is the cornerstone of Cognitive treatment. In contrast to the passive psychoanalyst in the Freudian school, the Cognitive therapist is much more active and directive. This Cognitive treatment method, referred to as Rational Emotive Therapy, or RET, was promoted by Albert Ellis.

During Cognitive therapy I challenge what the client is saying/thinking. I point out the illogic in their statements. For example, recently I saw a client who was dumped by her boyfriend and she lamented, "I will never find my true love." I responded with something like, "I understand you're upset, but to tell yourself that because one man left you, there is no other man in the universe who may come to love you, makes no sense. Now, if you continue to think—and act—like there is no man out there for you, your negative, irrational thinking just may come true."

To further encourage clients to question their faulty thinking, I also often ask them questions like:

"Did all that worrying help?"

"What's the worst thing that could happen?"

"When you think that way, how would you expect to feel?"

Another Simplification

I simplified the notion of the **unconscious**, in the Analytic view, in terms of **Truths** we develop in our childhood to make the concept more comprehensible and palatable to clients. By the same token, to make the notion of the **Self** a bit easier to understand, I refer, instead, to our "**inner coach**." (My apologies to dyed-in-the wool Cognitivists.) Some of us have a "coach" who is kind, gentle, and supportive. This coach inspires, guides, encourages, praises, and challenges us. It tells us, "You can do it—try again; better luck next time," when we fall. On the other hand, some of us have, unfortunately, an inner coach who is stern, rough, and intolerant. This coach discourages, is pessimistic, demeans, tears us down, and when we fall, tells us, "I told you so; you can't do it; why do you even try?"

These negative messages from our "inner coach" that many people "hear" are like re-circulating "tapes" that continually run in our head. Therefore, while the goal of therapy in the Cognitive view is to change your thinking, another way I like to look at it is that the goal of Cognitive treatment is to "fire your negative coach and hire a more positive one."

A Few Examples

Recently I had a new patient scheduled at noon. At about 11:40 am my secretary informed me that my new client would be late because she just called and said she was parked at the side of the road nearby with a flat tire and was awaiting the AAA truck.

The new client arrived about 12:20 pm. Her hair was somewhat askew and a black smudge, presumably from a tire, was evident on her cheek.

When I ushered her into the office, she immediately apologized for being late and then said, "I can't believe I had a flat tire."

Wanting to validate her concerns but yet stay reality-based, I replied, "Having a flat tire is always a nuisance; there is never a convenient time to have one. Unfortunately, with all the construction going on in the Valley, with nails and debris on the roads, flat tires are fairly common."

Despite my comment, she next said, "My day is ruined!"

Again, attempting to be empathetic yet real, I said something like, "I can understand how this morning may not have been your best, but it is only about noon now and you have the rest of the day to make today a good one."

The client continued, "This kind of thing happens to me all the time!"

I replied, "I understand that you are currently upset but flat tires occur commonly and randomly in the Valley."

Finally, she concluded, "Everything I touch just turns to crap! I can't seem to do anything right!"

I responded, "I don't believe having a flat tire means you are a failure as a person."

Within ten to 15 minutes I had her diagnosis. This woman was engaging in such protracted negative thinking she had to be feeling miserable emotionally. She clearly was quite depressed.

The DSM-IV (Diagnostic and Statistical Manual-4th Edition), published by the American Psychiatric Association, lists all the mental health conditions known to mankind. It characterizes depression as a "mood disorder," obviously following the medical model or Biological school of thought. In the Cognitive view, though, depression is not considered a mood disorder but rather is seen as a **thinking** disorder. When you regularly say negative, pessimistic things, it strongly suggests you are thinking in a similarly negative, self-defeating manner.

Brian and Panic Attacks

Last year I saw Brian, 28, five or six times for panic disorder. He progressed quickly and was moved to a once-a-month appointment basis in preparation for termination. Nevertheless, Brian scheduled an appointment only a few days after his last session.

When Brian came into the office he sat down and immediately stated, "Doc, I really had a bad one the other day."

I asked Brian to tell me more. He reported that the day before yesterday he was working but then some old symptoms returned—tightening of the chest and his throat began to close. He stated, "Although those symptoms weren't new, they seemed a bit more intense than normal. It dawned on me that if my chest continued to tighten and my throat closed, I could die. I then proceeded to have one of the worst panic attacks in over a year."

I asked Brian, "How many panic attacks have you had in your life?"

Brian answered, "You know, Doc, a hundred or more."

I said, "If you were going to die from a panic attack, don't you think you'd be dead by now?"

He responded, "Doc, you're right. I see your point."

Finally, I asked, "What do you think you did to yourself when you entertained the thought that the symptoms you were having were possibly dangerous, even lethal?"

Since Brian had already previously worked with me he answered, "I see, Doc, I really thought myself into a bad one."

I took out an index card and printed the following:

"I'm having the early signs of a panic attack. I'm very familiar with these symptoms, as I have had many such panic attacks before. I know they are uncomfortable but not dangerous. If I breathe calmly and evenly and walk, I can minimize the symptoms."

I gave the index card to Brian and told him to fold it and place it in his wallet and carry it with him at all times. At the first sign of any panic, he should pull out the card and read it—preferably aloud. He replied, "Thanks, Doc, this should help." I saw Brian for three or four more times on a monthly basis and then successfully terminated with him.

The above is an example of classic cognitive therapy. I helped Brian recognize that his thinking that his symptoms were dangerous was unfounded and anxiety-producing. By giving him the index card he could now "change the script" the next time he began to have any panic symptoms and reduce the severity of the episode or possibly head it off entirely.

Michelle and Test Anxiety

Several months ago I saw Michelle, 16, due to "test anxiety." Her parents reported that Michelle is a very conscientious student and earned excellent grades until she entered high school. She then began "bombing tests" her freshman year and has not stopped. She still gets A's on her homework and projects but ends up with a B or C in the class because she does poorly on tests and exams.

When I met with Michelle we chatted for a bit. She was clearly intelligent, caring, but rather tense. I asked her, "What are you thinking when you sit down to take an exam?"

Initially, she was not certain what to say but finally she got it. She said, "I tell myself, I **hate** tests! I **always** fail them! I **never** can demonstrate how much I have learned. It **always** is **terrible**."

Initially, I helped Michelle understand that when she is about to take a test and tells herself she is about to embark on something that she "hates" and likely will "fail" at, she is essentially telling her brain that she is under attack. It is as if she was asking her brain to focus, reflect, and concentrate, at the same time she is fighting off a pack of hungry wolves. It can't be done.

I then asked Michelle, "What is the 'terrible' part?"

She said, "You know, the failure."

I then said, "You have failed many times already, so what's so terrible? Does your teacher parade your exam with an F on it around the room? Do your friends stop speaking to you? Do your parents stop loving you?"

She answered "No" to all of the above.

I then said, "You are telling yourself that getting an F on a test is "terrible," but obviously it is not. Getting an F may not be fun but it is not **terrible**. Besides, you have had many F's before and nothing **terrible** has occurred."

I pointed out to Michelle that she is "catastrophizing"—telling herself a situation is "terrible" when in fact it is only unpleasant. If you think something is terrible, it feels terrible. If you think something is unpleasant, it doesn't feel quite so bad.

I suggested that Michelle consider a new "script" to tell herself before she takes a test:

"I'm about to take a test. Tests are unpleasant for me but they are not terrible. I have failed tests before and nothing bad has happened. I know I have studied and I am prepared. I will do my best and whatever happens, happens."

Michelle made a sincere effort to change her thinking. By the end of the school year she was performing satisfactorily on tests.

Heather and "Tanking"

A few years ago a couple came in to see me regarding their adolescent daughter who was on the high school tennis team. They reported that Heather was the number one player on the team. She always played strongly when ahead but frequently lost close matches. They asked if I thought I could help her. Having played some tennis in my time and having a pretty good idea what was going on in this case, I said, "Yes I think I can help."

Heather was a bright, athletic, motivated teen who was a pleasure to work with. It did not take long for Heather to comprehend that thinking led to feelings which results in behavior—which can confirm the original thinking. She quickly came to understand that in a close match she was negatively coaching herself by thinking the following:

"My opponent is trying really hard. Her shots are getting stronger. She is trying harder to get to everything. I could lose. That would be horrible."

Heather said, "I get it but what should I do?"

I started working with Heather by saying, "I read somewhere that in all of the tennis matches ever played, fifty percent of the time someone loses."

Heather laughed.

My goal here was to get Heather to recognize that failure, now and then, is inevitable. It is not that we welcome it, but we sometimes have to accept it. In sports—and in life—we are likely to now and then compete with someone who is more talented than us. Not everyone can be a Michael Jordan. Yet even Michael Jordan and his team lost a game now and then.

I continued, "The objective in sports—and life—is to play your best game. If you are defeated by someone better than you, then accept it—in fact, learn from it. In sports and life you learn more from playing and competing with people who are better than you. It may feed your ego to 'bagle' your opponent in a tennis set (win the set 6 to 0) but such a set will probably do little to improve your tennis game.

"What you don't want to do is to lose to an opponent who is less talented than you. When you start that 'stinking thinking' when your opponent tries harder you begin to feel tense, and you develop 'concrete elbow' (where you shorten your swing and hit the ball short, or into the net). As you become more anxious and passive, your opponent becomes more confident and aggressive. In sports (and life) this is called "choking" or "tanking."

I recommended that Heather tell herself the following:

"This is a tennis match, not a life or death match like with two gladiators in the Roman Coliseum. It is inevitable that my opponent is going to try harder, especially at the end of the match. If she is better than me then so be it, but she will have to beat me at my best game. I will take a deep breath, relax, focus on clearing the net (as statistically that's where most errors in tennis occur), and hit my best shots."

Heather benefitted from our work. She won State that year (her senior year) and went on to college on a tennis scholarship. I guess one of the reasons I enjoy sports so much is because much of sports is like life.

Even Therapists Sometimes Engage in "Stinkin Thinkin"

Recently, I finished with my 11:00 am client and walked into the office kitchen to get my lunch. There stood Jill, one of our part-time therapists, reading a letter. Out loud she stated, "My gosh! If this keeps up I won't have any clients left."

Since I was standing there, I said, "Jill, what's up?"

She handed me the note. It was from a client asking that Jill send her treatment notes to another therapist in Chandler (the other side of the Valley).

I said to Jill, "This is strange that your client wants her record sent to a therapist nearly 50 miles away."

With that Jill said, "You know, that reminds me; my client did say in the last session that she was thinking of moving to the East Valley."

I then said, "Now that makes more sense. Your client is moving far away from this office. You started treatment with her, which she enjoys and has benefitted from, and she wants to continue in treatment with another therapist now more conveniently located."

Jill reacted, "Larry, thanks, I really **feel** better now."

Jill had taken a simple note from a client asking that her records be sent to another therapist to mean that:

1. She was a poor therapist;
2. She had failed with this client; and
3. If this continues, she would have no practice left and be out on the street.

Of course, all of this was pure "stinkin thinkin." Even mental health professionals are not immune from thinking in an unhealthy manner now and again.

"I'll Concern Myself With It When I have To."

I have seen many clients who spend an inordinate amount of time worrying. Initially, they tell me they "can't help it" or "it is what I've always done" or "I was born this way." I don't believe we are born to worry (a Biological explanation) but rather we **learn** to **think** in such a manner (a Cognitive view). Worrying takes a lot of time and energy. When we worry, our body reacts like we are under attack (called "fight/flight"). Excessive worrying can make us sick, shorten our life, and leaves us without the emotional and physical stamina to properly address our problems. Thus, once again, we are "**stuck**."

Recently, I had a case where this 60-year-old gentleman, Warren, was dreading the impending marriage of his step-daughter back east. He said, "I haven't seen my step-daughter in years. I haven't had contact with my ex-wife in over a decade. I am really, really not looking forward to seeing all my ex-in-laws and ex-relatives. Besides, I hate to fly—especially long distances."

Warren said that he had lost many nights' sleep ruminating about how unpleasant this experience was going to be. The second time I saw Warren, about two weeks later, he said he endured a two-day bout of diarrhea, thinking about the event. Two-three weeks later he noted he spent several days in bed with a migraine that he was certain was caused by his anguish about this up-coming wedding. A few weeks later his back went out for several days.

When the wedding date was nigh, I asked Warren to set another appointment as soon as possible upon his return to discuss the trip. Three days after returning home from the long-feared wedding, Warren entered my office. I immediately asked, "Well, how did it go?"

Warren replied, "You know, it wasn't as bad as I thought. I actually had a pretty good time."

I have heard many clients tell me, "It wasn't as bad as I expected," because they were "catastrophizing" in the first place. Now, can Warren learn from this?

Warren wanted to move onto another topic, but I stopped him. "Warren, what about those sleepless nights, the diarrhea, that migraine and the back problem? Look at all the suffering you put yourself through. Was it all worth it? Did worrying help the situation? What can you learn from this?"

Warren agreed he needed to "learn to not worry—unless I have to" (at least a partial success).

While writing this book Nan and I purchased an income property. About a week after we closed on the property, on a Friday evening, at about 6 pm, Nan and I came home at about the same time and I brought in the mail. As I was putting something away, I overheard Nan say, as she was opening the mail, "Oh, no! This isn't good!"

I quickly walked over to her and Nan showed me a letter from the headquarters of the escrow company. It noted a problem with the escrow on the house we just purchased and the loan may be due in full. Becoming upset, Nan said, "This is bad. We could lose the house and our down payment!"

I looked closely at the letter and said, "Dear, this letter came from an office in Jupiter, Florida. It is about 6:30 pm here in Arizona, so it is about 9:30 pm in Florida. I don't believe anyone is there to talk to us now. So, you can remain upset all weekend, worry, not sleep, not eat, cancel our social engagements, and then make a call Monday morning. Or, we can put this letter aside, enjoy our weekend, and then make a call Monday morning. You decide."

To which Nan said, "This is what I get for marrying a psychologist."

We put the letter aside and had a nice weekend. At 6:30 am Monday morning I called the escrow office in Florida and straightened the situation out in 15 minutes—before Nan awoke that morning.

Would worrying have helped the situation? I doubt it. It may have even worsened the problem because if I had allowed myself to worry all weekend, I might not have been mentally sharp enough to solve the problem on Monday morning. As I like to say—to myself, to my family, and to my patients—"I'll concern myself with it when I have to."

Managing Problems

I often tell clients that there are three basic healthy ways to deal with a problem:

1. Some problems can be fixed or resolved.

The essential element here is control. If you have the control and capacity to solve the problem, then do so. Unfortunately, I constantly see patients who are trying to fix problems about which they have no control. Trying to get your significant other to quit drinking or smoking, wishing your boss would treat you better, or insisting that your adolescent earns straight A's, are common examples.

2. Some problems can and should be left or avoided.

For example, if your boss is completely out of control, despite your best attempts to address the situation, you may well be best served by looking for another job (or starting your own small business). If your significant other is abusive, you should leave, at least until he or she has begun treatment.

3. If you cannot fix or avoid the problem, the only healthy remaining option is to find "acceptance."

Often, clients/patients come to me about someone (or something) in their life that is troubling them. In most cases that other person is not interested in coming into my office to discuss the problem; they may even be unaware that a problem exists. Nevertheless, many times my client leaves treatment "feeling" better. Did the other person or the situation change? In most cases no. What changed is how the client now perceives the problem.

4. What commonly causes people great angst is this last and most unhealthy choice, which I call the "I Can't Stand It!" position.

In this mode the individual essentially says himself or herself, "I have this problem. I do not have control of this issue so I can't fix it. I choose not to leave it. I will not accept it. So I choose to allow this problem to continue to agitate, stress, and aggravate me—hence, "I Can't Stand It!"

For all intents and purposes, what I am referring to here is the "Serenity Prayer," first offered by Reinhold Niebuhr in the 1940's:

"God, grant me the serenity to accept the things I cannot change,
The courage to change the things I can,
And the wisdom to know the difference."

This refrain is often said at AA meetings, but it clearly does not apply only to alcoholism; it applies to life in general. Obviously it stems from a Cognitive perspective.

The Power to Choose Your Feelings

Understanding and implementing Cognitive psychology, I believe, is empowering. Since we think before we feel—"Cognition before emotion"—we essentially can **choose** our feelings. Many of us though, unfortunately, do not live this way. How often do we think—say to ourselves—or hear someone say:
"He/she made me mad."
"He/she hurt my feelings."
"He/she is driving me crazy!"
These statements imply that someone caused you, forced you, to feel a certain way. Notice that in each of the above three statements something physical is suggested:
You were **made** to become angry, your feelings were **bruised**, and, lastly, someone's behavior **drove** you to become upset.
These implications are false on two fronts:

First, this process is psychological, not physical.

Second, no one makes us feel anything. It is our **choice**. We cannot control what others say or do to us, but we can control how we choose to **feel** about it. (If someone jumps out from behind a bush and flourishes a knife, obviously you will feel terror—unless, perhaps you are well-versed in self defense. Fortunately, such traumatic events are rare and the ability to choose one's feeling applies well to daily life.)

I believe it was Mark Twain who said well over a hundred years ago:

"Stress is not what happens to you; stress is what you make of what happens to you."

Similarly, Eleanor Roosevelt is often quoted to have said, "No one can make you feel inferior without your consent."

Again, being able to recognize that you, in large part, are in control of how you feel is empowering.

Cognitively-Based Questions I Often Ask Clients

When working with clients I often ask the following questions in the effort to help the client challenge and change their "stinkin thinkin" and put their thinking in the proper perspective:

"Will this be a big deal 24 hours from now?"

"Who won the Super Bowl last year?" (It was a huge deal then but few people remember it now.)

"Has all this worrying helped the situation?"

"Why not concern yourself with it when you need to?" (Instead of worrying endlessly about it)

"Who did you kill today?" (Because some people feel so guilty it is like they killed someone.)

Will I read about this in the newspaper? (Is it really that important?)

"What's the worst thing that could happen?" (It usually has already occurred.)

"Hasn't the worst thing already happened?"

While in the process of writing this chapter, I had a client who told me, "I got this big medical bill in the mail yesterday and was so upset I didn't sleep a wink last night."

I asked her, "So when you finally got out of bed this morning, was your bill any less? Did the worrying help?"

She wryly smiled and said, "I get it."

Again, the purpose of these questions is to start a conversation, to help clients realize the lack of logic in their thoughts, help them understand how this negative and illogical thinking hurts them, and to get the clients to think in a more positive, logical, healthy manner.

Some of the Signs of a Fragile Self— or Low Self-Image

Below are common symptoms of poor self-esteem:

1. Feeling like a failure and believing you can never be successful

2. Focusing on the negative in just about any situation

3. Being totally adverse to any criticism, regardless how constructive

4. Regularly needing approval

5. Setting unrealistic expectations at which you are almost certain to fail

6. Resenting the achievements and successes of others

7. Putting yourself down—publicly and privately

8. Being a braggart

9. Worrying excessively

10. Constantly comparing ourselves to others

According to the Cognitive model, these negative forms of thinking significantly contribute to emotional discomfort, failure, and, once more, keep us "stuck."

What to Do

The cognitive model suggests several ways to achieve your life goals:

1. Begin a Personal Journal

Journaling is an excellent method to learn to identify and change your distorted thinking. On a daily basis, or at least several times a week, you should note your experiences and journal your thoughts and resultant feelings. By doing this you will quickly come to recognize your "stinkin thinkin" and the need to replace your unhealthy thinking with rational, real, healthy thoughts. You will become able to identify when you are catastrophizing, worrying excessively, lying to yourself, making excuses, and/or putting yourself down. As you recognize these things, you can write your new goals and objectives. It is always instructive to reread your journal and realize how far you have come in achieving healthy thinking.

2. Learn New Affirmations

As you know by now, according to the Cognitive model, what you tell yourself determines what you feel, which directs how you behave. It should make perfect sense, then, that if you want to make positive changes, you must learn to tell yourself new positive things. We do this by using **affirmations**. Affirmations are simple, positive, self-statements that you repeat and practice. The objective of affirmations is that these new, positive, healthy, supportive, statements become integrated into your **Self**-system. (Your new, positive inner "Self-coach.")

Below are a number of classic positive affirmations with which many people can benefit:

"I believe in myself!"

"I can expect great things in life."

"I can accomplish anything I set my mind to."

"I deserve love, happiness, and success."

"I view challenges not as "stumbling blocks" but as an opportunity ("stepping stones") to improve myself and grow as a person."

"I will take action whenever an opportunity presents itself."

"I will take a step toward my dream every day."

"I am grateful for all the positive things in my life."

"I am a unique and talented individual with much to offer."

"I will invest in myself."

The above are just a few of the basic affirmations most people can use. Of course, you might want to write down some of your own affirmations, specific to your situation. You can always add, delete, or change one.

3. Remove Negative Self-Statements

While you are in the process of making the above positive self-statements, you also will need to begin removing your negative thoughts. Make a list of your long-held negative self-statements that you have been telling yourself for some time that have been dragging you down and keeping you "stuck." Consider asking your spouse or best friend if they have any suggestions of negative self-comments you commonly make or imply which you should discard.

Look at each and every negative self-statement, challenge them, and vow not to repeat them to yourself again. Replace each negative statement with a corresponding positive one. For example, suppose one of your regular negative self-thoughts was: "Everything I touch usually turns to failure." You can change that statement to:

"From now on everything I do will be successful."

Changing your "thinking habits" will not happen overnight. You likely will catch yourself, now and then, considering a negative statement. You, then, will have to stop yourself and restate that comment, preferably aloud, in a positive manner.

I recommend that you write, even type your positive affirmations on a sticky note or on index card and attach these cards to your bathroom mirror, kitchen table, bedroom mirror, and even your calendar at work. In this manner, several times per day, you will now read, and hopefully even say aloud, your new positive self-statements. As noted previously, you now can fire your negative personal coach and hire your new positive one.

4. "Walk the Talk"

As you go through the process of deleting negative self-statements and integrating positive statements into your Self-structure, you want to ensure that you are making every effort to **do** what you now think—"walk the talk." For example, if one of your affirmations is "I will take action whenever an opportunity presents itself," if an opportunity does, in fact, come your way, you **must** make that phone call, send that letter or e-mail—and follow up!

5. According to the Cognitive "Law of Attraction"—which essentially says you get what you believe you deserve—it becomes extremely important to Set Goals.

The goals should be stated in a positive, fairly **specific** manner. They should be short-term and **achievable**. The purpose of this goal-setting is to help you focus on and accomplish particular objectives which lead you to even larger objectives.

Below are examples of certain goals you may care to set:

In the effort to improve my relationship with my wife, I will not lose my temper this week.

Next Saturday I will fix that cabinet door I have been promising to do for some time.

Next Saturday morning I will take my son out for breakfast. On Sunday morning I will take him to the park (to fish, feed the ducks, and/or play in the sandbox).

This week I will put a little "love note" in my spouse's lunchbox or purse.

At least twice this week I will rub my wife's back in bed and not ask for or expect sex in return.

At least twice this week I will read a bed-time story to my child (children).

By Saturday I will take out a trial membership at the Y or the gym and have the trainer show me how to organize a workout and use some of the equipment.

For this week I will start every morning with a brisk walk around the block—twice (and I will encourage a family member to come along with me).

With my next pay check I will open a separate account at the bank and place $100.00 in it. This money, and other money I will add to it, will only be used for investing or funding an IRA.

This month I will only purchase something if I can pay cash for it or have sufficient funds in my checking account to write a check or use my credit card.

I will enroll in a college class and/or in a class on investing by the start of next semester.

When grocery shopping this week I will purchase only nutritious and healthy foods.

I will call my doctor's office and ask if they have any information or recommended eating plans to healthfully lose weight.

The purpose of these relatively simple, short-term goals is to "get the ball rolling." We all need to get started and we need to start somewhere. As you know, just as negative thinking has led to negative feelings and negative behavior, we became stuck. On the other hand, positive thinking and positive goal-setting can lead to positive feelings and positive behaviors—and now we are moving forward and are growing. The ultimate purpose for goal setting is to determine and work toward accomplishing our larger life goals.

6. Visualization.

Once you have set a goal take the time to sit back, close your eyes, and visualize in your mind you accomplishing that goal. In sports psychology athletes are trained to visualize themselves throwing a perfect pitch, hitting that perfect golf shot, or running a perfect race. If it works for athletes, it can work for you.

Depending on your goals take the time to visualize the following:

Having a warm, loving relationship with your family members.

Exercising regularly and seeing yourself become stronger and healthier.

Eating nutritious foods and becoming healthier and trimmer.

Continuing to put funds into your investment account and seeing that balance continue to grow.

Investing wisely and safely and developing passive streams of income coming toward you.

Attending classes and earning that degree or certification you always dreamed of.

Writing that novel that has always been in your head.

Your mind is amazingly powerful. However, like any tool, it must be used appropriately. Your mind and your thoughts can make you ill or healthy, or make you poor or successful. Frankly, it is pretty much up to you. Understanding Cognitive psychology and using the above-described methods of journaling, adopting new positive affirmations and deleting old ones, setting goals, and visualization, you will be well on your way to achieving your life goals.

Important Points to Remember in Chapter Five

1. Proponents of the Cognitive view argue that how you think determines how you feel, which ultimately determines how you behave. The system works either way: Positive thinking leads to positive feelings, which leads to positive behavior. However, negative thinking leads to negative feelings, which results in negative behavior.

2. According to Cognitive theory, good mental health is essentially healthy thinking (self-talk); poor mental health consists of negative, and destructive thinking—"stinkin thinking." Treatment takes the form of changing your thoughts (your Self-structure or self-esteem).

3. We all possess our "inner coach." Some of us have a positive, supportive one. Unfortunately, many of us have a negative, critical one. Many of us need to "fire our old coach and hire a new positive one."

4. Problems can be managed by fixing them, leaving them, or accepting them; avoid the "I can't stand it!" position. Remember the "Serenity Prayer."

5. No one makes us feel anything. We cannot control what others say or do but we have the power to choose how we feel about it.

6. We can use Cognitive psychology to achieve our life goals by way of journaling, learning new affirmations, removing negative self-statements from our Self, doing what we now think, and properly setting and visualizing our goals.

CHAPTER SIX

The Behavioral View

"It is far easier to behave your way into a new feeling than to feel your way into a new behavior."

The Behavioral school originated in the USA in the early 1900's. Early Behavioral pioneers were E.L. Thorndike, John Watson, and Joseph Wolpe. Unquestionably, Behavioral psychology was popularized by B. F. Skinner at Harvard in the 1940's. Like the Cognitive school, the Behavioral school is considered a contemporary model because the focus is on the present. Also like the Cognitive view, the Behavioral model is not as fatalistic as the Biological and Analytic schools and argues that individuals can readily change.

Behavioral psychology is focused on how the individual behaves—acts. The Biological view contends that behavior is the result of your genes and physiology; the Analytic model purports that behavior is due to the Truths gleaned from your childhood; and the Cognitive school notes that behavior is simply the end result of your thinking and subsequent feeling. Behaviorists, on the other hand, assert that studying how you behave, in and of itself, is critical and essential in understanding how you function. According to Behavioral theory, what is most important is behavior—not your biology, childhood, or thinking.

Behavioral psychology has been criticized as "black box psychology," because what is going on within the brain is considered insignificant; the brain is just a "black box." In response, Behaviorists criticize the Cognitive view that changing your thinking changes the problem. Behaviorists argue that understanding the cause of the problem and/or recognizing your thinking about the problem often does not correct the problem. For instance, how many people know why they smoke and recognize how they think (and feel) about the smoking, but continue to engage in the bad habit?

Skinner's research indicated that most behavior is "learned"—initially by trial and error. According to Skinner, nearly every behavior is followed by one of three consequences: a positive result—**reinforcement**; a negative result—**punishment**; or a neutral result—**extinction**. This pattern of consequences "shapes" the individual's characteristic pattern of behaving. Behaviors that have a positive consequence—that receive positive reinforcement—tend to be repeated. Behaviors that engender a negative consequence—punishment—generally lead to avoidance. Behaviors that result in neutral consequences—extinction—tend to drop out.

The effect of every consequence—positive, negative, or neutral—is unique to that individual. For example, a young child who receives little or no attention from his father may learn to irritate his father, which causes his father to yell at him. For most individuals having their parent scold them would be perceived as a negative (or punishing) consequence, but for this child, who is striving for attention, getting his father to acknowledge and pay attention to him is, in fact, a positive (reinforcing) consequence.

According to the Behavioral view, learning can be adaptive or maladaptive. For example:

A toddler asks his mother for a cookie shortly before dinner. Mother says, "No, Timmy, it's close to supper time; a cookie will spoil your appetite." Timmy again asks for a cookie and again Mother denies the request. After two more requests and two more denials, Timmy, now frustrated, flops to the floor (is about to have a temper tantrum) and screams (for the fourth time), "I want a cookie!" Not wanting to witness another emotional outburst, Mother relents and says, "Okay, have your darn cookie!"

In this example (which occurs thousands of times across the USA every day) both Mother and child learned something—and the learning is not particularly adaptive: The child learned that if he is persistent and threatens to tantrum, he stands a good chance of getting what he wants. Thus, in the future, when the child asks for something and Mother says "No," as far as Timmy is concerned, "We're just getting started!" Despite its effectiveness in this case (in obtaining a cookie), learning to be obnoxious and oppositional are clearly not adaptive characteristics to learn and practice in the community.

Mother learned that if she capitulates when Timmy is about to throw a temper tantrum, she can prevent the outburst. (Technically this is called negative reinforcement.) Of course, giving into Timmy's demands, especially before he is about to have a meltdown, is clearly self-defeating. Obviously, more oppositional behavior and temper tantrums are likely to occur.

Timmy learned that he had to request a cookie several times before he finally received one. This exemplified a concept called **intermittent reinforcement**. Behaviors that are rewarded on an intermittent basis occur at high rates and are very difficult to remove. Gambling casinos understand and use this notion well.

Interestingly, if you were to interview Mother and ask why Timmy behaves in this manner she might very well say any of the following:

"He was born that way"—a Biological exclamation.

"He takes after his uncle"—another genetic/Biological exclamation.

"I think I weaned him too early and he fought me during toilet training"—an Analytic explanation.

"Once he gets a thought in his head he just won't let it go"—a Cognitive explanation.

The best explanation of Timmy's behavior, though, is that Mother and the environment she presents to Timmy have trained him to behave in this manner. According to Behaviorists, Timmy's behavior is predictable.

Must Feel Like It to Do It

How many times do you hear people say they didn't do something they set out to do or were supposed to do because they "didn't **feel** like it?" These individuals are operating on the premise that they have to be in a certain **mood state** before they can **do** something. In other words, they first have to **feel** it and then, and only then, can they **do** it.

Behaviorists argue that waiting until the "feeling" arises to do something is foolish and a waste of time. Behaviorists contend that waiting to feel like doing something before you do it is backward: If you do something, you likely will feel differently about it. If the task is worth doing, you should do it. Borrowing from the Nike ad:

"Just do it!"

Social psychologists, for example, have known for years that many individuals maintain prejudices against persons of certain races or ethnicities, yet most of these bigoted people did not even know someone who belongs to the disparaged race or ethnicity. Data has shown that if bigoted people are given the opportunity to get to know some individual against whom they were biased, many of these bigoted individuals will change their views. Thus, a change of behavior (getting to interact with a minority individual, for example) can lead to a change in feeling (a change in racial prejudice).

Recently, my alarm clock went off at 5:30 am on a dark cold Friday morning, so that I could prepare to go to the gym and do my aerobic workout. As I shut off the alarm, Nan said, "Oh, it's so dark and cold; don't you feel like just staying in this warm cozy bed?" (I thought for a moment I was receiving an invitation, but I was wrong.)

I answered, "Yes," but proceeded to prepare to go to the gym. After I put on my workout clothes, packed my work clothes to change into, packed my lunch, and ate my breakfast, I went back into the bedroom and said goodbye to Nan before I left.

Upon saying goodbye, Nan said, "I thought you said you felt like staying in bed."

I answered, "Yes, I did say I felt like staying in bed this morning but you know, dear, I live according to what I must **do;** not according to what I **feel**."

Nan shrugged her shoulders, rolled over, and went back to sleep.

Fifteen minutes later I was at the gym riding the stationary bike. How did I feel about being there, then? Great! Notice that in this example I ignored my feelings, forced the behavior, and subsequently felt differently—and good about it. This little scenario points out a basic behavioral maxim:

"It is far easier to behave your way into a new feeling than to feel your way into a new behavior." Those who wait to **feel** like regularly going to the gym, rarely get there.

"Get Around to It"

With respect to the notion that people have to be in a certain feeling state before they can do something, is that many people put things off—procrastinate—presumably until they finally reach that particular mood condition that allows them to do whatever it is they should. In treatment sessions I usually hear such individuals say they will accomplish some task, when they "get around to it." Whenever I hear that phrase I reach into my desk drawer and hand them a clear glass ball with the letters TUIT inscribed on it. When the patient inevitably asks me, "What is this?" I answer, "You said you were waiting 'to get around to it' so now you have it—a round TUIT. So let's do it!"

The point of this little trick, of course, is to illustrate to clients that they are simply putting off what they should **do**. Now that they have their "TUIT," they should go about achieving their goal. Again, we don't necessarily have to **feel** like doing something to **do** it.

Doing Depression

Last year I worked with a middle-aged woman who had struggled with depression her entire life. Joyce's first depressive episode occurred in her early teens. She noted that her mother and maternal grandmother also suffered with depression (so Biological issues were also clearly involved in this case). She reported that over the years she had seen "many, many physicians, including a number of psychiatrists." She tried "every antidepressant in the book." On occasion, she would see a therapist but little had changed.

Frustrated, Joyce lamented, "I take my medication as prescribed but I never feel good."

Joyce had "walking depression," as I sometimes call it, but technically it is referred to as Dysthymia. She could work, run her house, and do her activities of daily living (shop, clean, care for herself, and so on) and was not suicidal (at least not 98 percent of the time). On the other hand, she rarely felt happy, rarely did anything outside her job, and led an isolated existence.

Joyce worked as an English/drama teacher at a private school. She was responsible for putting on a school play in the spring and the fall. The school often used her plays as a marketing instrument to attract new students, as the community was always invited to the plays. Joyce liked her work and was good at it, but her job took so much of her energy she frequently came home from work, corrected a few papers, and went to bed by 7 pm, usually without dinner.

Having dealt with depression for more than three decades, Joyce had, more or less, "given into" her illness. She had seen a dozen or so mental health professionals, had followed their recommendations, but saw little improvement. She came to me to "try once again" but clearly her expectations were low. Joyce presented a challenge.

At the third or fourth session I proposed this to her:

"Joyce, suppose you had to direct a new play in which the hero of the play was depressed. How would you stage it?"

Immediately, I saw that Joyce got into this concept, as she wiggled in her seat a bit, and said, "Let's see. First, I would have her (Joyce made the hero a female) walk around in her housecoat (bathrobe) with her hair in curlers. I would have one of the curlers hang down from her head for dramatic effect."

I said, "Okay, I think that's a good start. What else?"

Joyce said, "Well, I would stage the apartment to be dark— with the TV on in the corner—but I would shine lights on the shades from the outside the stage so the audience could see that it was bright outside but dark inside the apartment."

"All right," I said, "I think we are getting there. What else would you do?"

"Well, I'd have her move slowly and lay around a lot."

"Okay; that's good. Anything else?"

Joyce was getting a bit stuck, so I assisted, "Anything about what she might be eating?"

With that, Joyce said, "Okay; I would have her nuke some old coffee and an old dried sweet roll. Oh, I would also have her smoke a few cigarettes, too."

"Joyce, the audience would really begin seeing the picture that this woman was depressed," I next said, "How about something in the social arena?"

Joyce pondered the question for a moment and said, "Oh, I think a great scene would be that the phone would ring but, of course, she doesn't answer it. The caller hears the recorded message and then leaves her own message, "Judy, are you okay? This is my third call to you without a response. Please call me. Beeeeep."

I then said, "Joyce, I can see you are a great drama director. No question the audience would know this heroine was depressed."

At that moment, Joyce looked intensely at me and said, "Dr. Waldman, you tricked me!"

Innocently, I answered, "What do you mean?"

Joyce said, "I do these things."

I answered, "Yes, Joyce. We call this **doing depression**." I continued, "If someone who was previously happy was forced to live your lifestyle, what do you think they would be like in four weeks?"

Joyce replied, "Probably depressed."

"Yes," I said, "and they weren't depressed in the first place." I suggested to Joyce that depression cannot be treated like a cold. "Take your medicine, stay home, get lots of rest, and wait until you feel better. To get out of depression, you must **work** your way out.

You must sleep right, eat right, exercise right, socialize right, put sun on your face, and put a smile on your face."

Joyce answered, a bit sarcastically, "It sounds like you are saying, 'Fake it till you make it.'"

I answered, "Any Behaviorist would absolutely agree with you. Often clients tell me that when they feel better they will do some of the things I recommend. I correct them and suggest they have it backwards: When you do some of these things, you will feel better."

Numerous clinical studies have shown that experimental subjects who are depressed who begin and maintain a regular exercise program do as well, and sometimes even better, than subjects who receive only psychotherapy or medication. Exercising, sleeping right, eating right, socializing or smiling does not happen in a vacuum. By doing these things it affects the world around you differently, which in turn affects (reinforces) you differently, as well.

Joyce agreed to try. We set up a proper sleep and wake schedule, a proper eating routine, and an exercise program. She called her friend back and set up a couple of social engagements. She joined a bridge club. She signed up with an online dating site. Four months later, she reported, "Never remember ever feeling better."

Depression, from the Biological view, is essentially innate and requires medication. According to the Analytic perspective, depression stems from the unresolved issues of your childhood and is treated through long-term psychoanalysis. Per the Cognitive school, depression is essentially "stinkin thinkin" and is managed by cognitive retraining. Behaviorists, in contrast, argue that depression is learned. We give in to certain feelings and develop a characteristic set of maladaptive behaviors—sleeping too much or too little, eating too little (typically) or too much, becoming unmotivated and sedentary, choosing to let our general hygiene lapse and isolating socially. By **working** to reverse these behaveiors, as many studies have demonstrated, depression can be improved.

Behaving "As If"

Over the years I frequently have cases where a wife with marital problems comes into the office alone. She comes alone because her husband typically refuses to participate in marital counseling and believes the problem is all due to his wife, anyway. The wife says something like, "I love my husband; I'm just not in love with him." (Hence the title of my marriage book, *How Come I Love Him But Can't Live With Him?)*

After listening to the wife, I often say something like, "I wish I could whip up some 'love potion number nine' to help you regain that loving feeling." Of course, the wife smiles and recognizes that an elixir of some sort will not solve her problem. (Essentially, this is another example of someone wanting someone else to change to allow them to "feel" differently).

When the frustrated spouse asks me, then, "What should I do?" I then usually ask her, "What things can you do that you know that your husband would likely appreciate? For example, can you cook him his favorite dish, or rub his back, or agree to go to a ball game with him?"

After the wife lists a few things, she inevitably becomes skeptical and says something like, "Dr. Waldman, maybe you don't understand. I am here because I am unhappy, and frustrated, and have lost that loving feeling regarding my husband. Why are we talking about what I can do for him?"

At this point I explain, "You want to feel differently regarding your husband, but the only way that can happen is if your husband begins to behave differently toward you. He, unfortunately, is not here. You can talk to him and wait until he behaves differently toward you but you might have to wait a long time—maybe all the way into divorce court. On the other hand, you can immediately begin behaving differently toward him by doing things you know he likes and if there is anything left in the relationship, he likely will reciprocate by beginning to do things, in return, you like—and you will begin to feel differently and positively about him."

More often than not this works. Interestingly, frequently the husband subsequently enters the treatment process as well, since he comes to believe that I must know what I'm talking about because his wife "has never treated me better."

This is a prime example of "behaving as if." By encouraging the wife to behave **as if** she loved her husband, her positive behaviors toward her husband were reinforced with positive behaviors back. Clearly, as the wife became more frustrated in the marriage and began to lose her "loving feelings" toward her husband, she unquestionably began to exhibit behaviors that reflected her unhappiness—withdrawal and anger. In turn, her husband undoubtedly responded with similar negative behaviors— and the marriage turned cold.

Learning to "fake it till you make it," or behaving "as if," can be applied in many situations, and can be very powerful. Essentially, this concept relates to the distinctly Behavioral notion that our behavior does not occur in a vacuum. What behaviors we put out determine how others react to us:

"Garbage in, garbage out" per the techies; and "good behavior out and good behavior back," per Behavioral psychology.

Another Example—Josh and Mrs. G

At the very beginning of Josh's junior year in high school he reported at the dinner table one evening that he was not enjoying his World History class because his teacher, Mrs. G, was "really old, stodgy, and boring. All she does is stand there and lecture," he said. To make matters worse, he said, "This is the first class of the day and it's early. My assigned seat is right in front of her desk. I have to fight to keep awake and not fall asleep right in front of her."

As I listened to Josh describe the situation, I asked him, "Josh, how do you think things look to Mrs. G?"

Josh gave me that "deer in the headlights" look because as a typical egocentric adolescent, he never pondered what the situation might seem like to the other person.

Josh answered, "Dad, I'm not sure."

I responded, "Josh, think about it. She's up there trying to impart some information and half or more of the class look like they just rolled out of bed and wish they were still there. Moreover, the kid sitting right in front of her looks like he is bored out of his skull. How exciting of a teacher do you expect her to be at 7:45 am under those conditions?"

Josh said, "I guess maybe she's as turned off as I am. So what am I supposed to do about it?"

I said, "Josh, let's do an experiment. (Josh heard that term before.) From now on I want you to sit up straight in your seat; maintain eye contact with Mrs. G; nod at her when she makes a point; and smile when she attempts to crack a joke, regardless of how corny it may be. A few days from now at the end of the period, as you are about to leave the class, turn to Mrs. G and say, 'interesting class today, Mrs. G.' Finally, in a week or so, stop by her desk after class for a brief chat before running out of the room like you were just let out of a cage."

Josh answered, "Dad, that sounds a lot like brown-nosing to me."

"No," I said, "that's good (Behavioral) psychology."

About three weeks later, at the dinner table, Nan and I were talking about our impending trip to Australia. Josh interceded and said, "Mrs. G has been to Australia; she said it's really cool. She's been all over the world."

"Really," I said, "how do you know all this?"

"Well," Josh reported, "I did what you said. We're talking a lot after class. She's really an interesting person. I hope to travel like her someday." (Josh and his bride recently went to Thailand for ten days for their honeymoon.)`

At the end of the semester Josh earned an A in World History and said that class was his favorite. Did Mrs. G become more interesting or did Josh first behave as if she was? Cognitivists argue behavior is the result of thinking and feeling, but Behaviorists contend, as seen in this example, new behavior can lead to new thinking and feeling.

Theory of Mental Health

The Behavioral view of mental health is simply and pragmatically that mental health consists of the individual primarily learning and exhibiting adaptive behaviors.

Theory of Mental Illness

The Behavioral view of mental illness is, again, pragmatic and simple in that mental illness is the result of the individual learning and consistently exhibiting maladaptive behaviors.

Mental Health Treatment

Treatment according to the Behavioral view consists of a process referred to as **Behavior Modification**—a specific procedure to change maladaptive behavior.

Behavior Modification

Behavior modification is the formula Behaviorists use to change behavior. It consists of several consecutive steps:

1. Identify the "**Target Behavior**," specifically and measureably.

2. Baseline that "Target Behavior."

3. If necessary, break down the "Target Behavior" into its component steps—"**Approximations**" to the Target Behavior.

4. Determine reinforcement, extinction, and punishment variables, and the schedule in which they will be applied.

5. Implement the intervention and continue to monitor the "Target Behavior."

6. Evaluate the change in the Target Behavior and revise as necessary.

Step 1 in Behavior Modification:
Identify the Target Behavior

Appropriately identifying a Target Behavior can assist with goal-setting and also can be quite therapeutic. For example, over the years I have had dozens of parents in my office complain that their child is "incorrigible," "unmanageable," and "unresponsive to discipline."

These parents are quite frustrated. They often feel hopeless and helpless and they clearly have no direction as to what to do.

What I typically do in these cases is to listen carefully and then reflect several of their concerns regarding their child's functioning. When I get agreement that these areas are, indeed, problematic, I then ask, "On what area do you think you want to concentrate on first?"

When I get the answer to that question I then ask the following "**magic questions**":

If your child were not being "aggressive," (if that was the area the parent chose to address first), "**What would your child be doing? What would it look like? What would I see?**"

The purpose of these questions is to help the parent begin to see the final goal in behavioral terms. This provides the needed direction to move forward. The final identified Target Behavior, in this case, might be:

"Jacob will reduce/cease hitting and/or yelling at his sister in the home."

When the parents entered the first session they were confused, fatalistic, helpless, and directionless. At the conclusion of the first session, when the identified Target Behavior had been determined, the parents were focused, directed, had a plan, and (though Behaviorists don't like to talk about it) the parents also felt much more hopeful and optimistic. Obviously, this is highly therapeutic.

The identified Target Behavior becomes the focus of the Behavior Modification program. All the subsequent steps are aimed at moving the targeted behavior in the right direction. The identified Target Behavior moves the "manager" from concept-ualization to actualization—from thought to action.

Some people might question whether such a simple program aimed at reducing the number of times Jacob hits or yells at his sister in the home will be of much benefit. Jacob has many other issues. How will changing one piece of behavior make much of a difference—if any?

First, Behaviorists say, "You have to start somewhere." Additionally, experience and research finds that if Jacob is trained to cease striking and screaming at his sister, very frequently other behaviors change for the better as well. Essentially, Jacob learns, "It pays off to be good."

By the same token, if Mother and/or Father learn how to change Jacob's behavior with respect to his "aggression," they can—and will—use those same techniques to address Jacob's other concerns. Very often in my practice when one Target Behavior is realized and I ask the parents if they want to address another issue, the parents decline and indicates that many of the other issues have improved as well. Behaviorists refer to this phenomenon as "Generalization."

In my marriage book (*How Come I Love Him But Can't Live With Him?*) I write about how identifying a Target Behavior is most useful in working with couples. Many partners throw amorphous complaints at each other like, "You need to be more considerate," or "Why aren't you more affectionate?"

Usually the first response to such a statement is "I don't know what you're talking about. I'm as considerate (or affectionate) as the next person."

This usually results in an argument. The truth of the matter is no one here has defined their terms.

My recommendation is that when a spouse registers one of the above complaints, the best response is to ask, "Dear, if I were to be more considerate (or affectionate), **'What would you see?' 'What would it look like**?'" In this manner, a real productive discussion can ensue.

Another Example

Often I will ask a new adult client at the end of the first session, "If we are successful and we decide to conclude treatment, what will you be doing differently? What will we see? What will it look like?" As Steven Covey recommended in his popular book, *"The Seven Habits of Highly Effective People,"* you should begin with the end in mind.

Last year a young man in his late-20's came into my office for his first session. When we sat down and went through the initial pleasantries, I asked Steven what brought him to treatment. Steven said, "Doc, my self-esteem is on the floor."

I looked at Steven and said, "Well, man, let's pick it up."

Steven gave me a quizzical look. I asked Steven if his self-esteem were at the level he wanted it, "What would you be doing differently?"

Interestingly, Steven said, "Well, I would feel better about myself."

Although the question was aimed at inducing a behavioral response, Steven went with "feeling" response.

I persisted and again asked Steven if his self-esteem were at an appropriate level, what kinds of things would he be doing? This question finally began to elicit some behavioral notions: Steven then listed some things pertaining to making better food choices, becoming more conscious of his clothing, becoming more social, losing some weight, and getting in better shape. I reflected to Steven that if he did the things he listed, his self-esteem would very likely rise. Steven agreed that would definitely be the case.

I then asked Steven on which of the areas that he listed to "raise" his self-esteem did he wish to first concentrate. After a bit of discussion, Steven said he felt that the first area on which to focus was to lose some weight and get into better physical condition.

Hearing that I then said, "Okay, then what do you think would be your first step in accomplishing that objective?"

Steven replied, "I'm almost ashamed to admit it but across the street from my apartment is a gym that I have looked at for more than a year-and-a-half but I have never gone into it. I guess my first step would be to enter that gym, take a look around, sign up for a trial membership, and maybe get a workout or two, probably with a trainer."

I strongly reinforced his first step and summarized what Steven would do before our next session. Steven agreed. At that point I concluded the session.

Steven walked into the office with essentially no specific goal other than he wanted to "raise his self-esteem off the floor." He left my office after our first session with a specific plan and direction. I contend this was very therapeutic. In fact, I worked with Steven for several months and at the end of that time Steven's self-esteem was "clearly off the floor" due to his new-found productive, responsible behaviors.

And Another Example

Last year, John, an IT tech, in his mid-40's, came into my office because he was "feeling down." After some discussion his primary concern had to do with his job. John had received a very poor job performance rating which meant that he was in jeopardy of being terminated.

After John described his situation I asked what he intended to do to improve his work performance. He was unable to give me a clear response. I asked him if his performance review provided any direction for him. He emphatically stated, "No." I then asked him if he would bring in a copy of his performance review to our next session.

In the following session I reviewed his performance review and agreed with John that it, in fact, provided no direction as to how to improve his performance. The performance review was replete with generalities and platitudes. It had comments like:

"John needs to facilitate his projects."

"John needs to become more of a self-starter."

After reading the review I asked John if it were possible for him to meet with his manager and go over the review and try to elicit some specific performance objectives. John indicated that he was not at all interested in such a conference and did not feel that it would be of any benefit. Absent such a meeting, I suggested that what he could do was reframe each amorphous comment in behavioral terms. He then could provide a behavioral goal which he would strive to accomplish by the next performance review. John liked the idea and said he would bring in a draft next session.

The following session John came with his response to his performance review. He did a great job. He listed eight vague points and nicely restated them in behavioral terms. He then noted his behavioral objectives (like sales figures and new accounts opened), which were observable and measurable, and the timeframes in which he would complete them. I praised John for his work and encouraged him to submit his response to his performance review.

In our following session John appeared much brighter than I had ever seen before. He noted that two days after he submitted his review response he received a call from the secretary of the CEO of the company asking him to come in for a meeting. At first, John felt apprehensive and thought that he was about to be terminated. However, when he met with the CEO the CEO indicated that he was most impressed by what John had done and said something like, "We need this. All my managers must learn to write their reviews in this manner."

The end result was that John had his review changed from less than satisfactory to a top ranking, he received a bonus, and he was also asked to train the managers about how to write more effective and instructive performance reviews. Again, effectively identifying a Target Behavior is quite useful.

Examples of Target Behaviors

Beginning with the next paycheck and for the next nine paychecks I will put five percent into a separate investment fund and another five percent into a separate vacation fund.

By Friday I will contact the American Cancer Society and find a smoking cessation program. By the end of the month I will have enrolled in one of those programs.

Beginning this Monday, for the next two weeks, I will limit myself to one (diet) soda per day. After two weeks I will allow myself three sodas per week. After that I will not drink soda, except for a rare, special occasion, no more than three times per month.

Beginning immediately, I will ensure that I am home from work by six o'clock and be certain that I read a bedtime story to my child at least four evenings per week.

Beginning immediately I will praise my spouse for something she or he has been doing positively for me or the family whenever I see that behavior.

By the end of this month I will plan a surprise "date night" with my spouse, including arranging for the babysitter.

By the end of next week I will edit and update my resume and have my spouse and best friend review it.

For the next six weeks, beginning this Monday. I will go to the gym on Mondays, Thursdays, and Saturdays, for one hour, to include 20 minutes of aerobic training, 40 minutes of resistance training, and 20 minutes of stretching.

Beginning today when I walk outside with my spouse I will hold her hand.

It should be noticed that the goals stated above have start dates and specific behaviors that can be observed and measured. Some goals have end dates. End dates do not mean that once you achieve their goal you should stop improving and return to your old, ineffective ways. No, you should continue to improve and perhaps move onto another goal.

According to behaviorists, once you behave in such a manner that you are receiving positive reinforcement for it, that behavior begins to sustain itself.

Behavioral objectives should be achieved one at a time. The old saying "Rome wasn't built in a day" is true. Trying to change too many behaviors at one time will decrease your chances of success. As one new goal becomes incorporated into your behavioral repertoire, you can take on a new one.

Step 2 in Behavior Modification:
Baselining

Once the Target Behavior is defined the next step is to baseline it. To Baseline means to take note of the status or rate of the Target Behavior before anything is done to modify it. Baselining is typically used when someone is trying to change someone else's behavior—like a parent altering a child's behavior, a spouse attempting to modify his or her partner's behavior, or a manager improving an employee's behavior. Baselining could also be used by an individual who is attempting to change his or her own behavior.

In the example previously noted, where the Target Behavior was to reduce the number of times Jacob is aggressive with his sister, a brief Baseline period of only a day or two would be used before any intervention was instituted, during which the parents would note how many times Jacob hit or yelled at his sister. Thus, a starting point would be identified. With more benign Target Behaviors, where someone is not at risk of being hit, a baseline period of a week is typical.

If interested in trying to lose some weight, for instance, an obvious baseline would be the individual's beginning weight before any kind of intervention is applied. If attempting to quit smoking, a baseline would likely include how many cigarettes are smoked each day for a week, at what time of the day, and what the person is feeling at the time he or she smoked each cigarette.

Baselining, therefore, provides a starting and a comparison point. Psychotherapy is frequently criticized as being inexact and amorphous. It is difficult, at times, to document the overall benefit of the psychotherapeutic process. However, using the Behavioral model, if the therapist has the client note the exact starting point with respect to a particular behavior before treatment and compares that baseline behavior to the frequency and intensity of that behavior upon concluding treatment, a clear indication of progress—or not—can be documented.

In addition to being able to verify progress, Baselining also helps in the area of managing your perspective. It has been my experience that when I assign someone to Baseline a family member's behavior—a child or a spouse—invariably that person returns and reports that the "misbehavior" was not, in fact, occurring as often as the person felt it was. This phenomenon is so universal I almost use it as a check to assess whether the individual did the Baseline homework. By recognizing that the problem is not as serious as he or she sensed it was, the person already begins to feel more optimistic—and therapy is already underway.

On a practical level, Baselining can also be part of the therapy—though traditional Behaviorists do not typically acknowledge that. Although I instruct clients to do nothing different during the baseline phase (which again can last for a day or two up to a week), I recognize that doing nothing different is unlikely. For instance, in the above case where Jacob was attacking his sister, what likely was happening was that when Jacob would confront his sister, his sister typically would yell and scream, and Mother and/or Father probably entered the scene and directed all their attention to Jacob, by scolding and yelling at him. By being instructed to simply baseline these incidents and do nothing different, the parent is likely to simply note the incident and not intervene as vigorously as before. This reduced attention provided to Jacob following his attacks on his sister may well begin to reduce the number and intensity of such incidents. (Behaviorists refer to this as "Extinction.") Baselining, therefore, sometimes can be therapeutic in and of itself.

Step 3 in Behavior Modification:
Approximations to Behavior

Some target behaviors may be too complex for the individual to achieve at once. For example, if your target behavior is to run a half-marathon by the end of the year but you cannot currently run around the block, clearly the goal of running a half-marathon must be broken into its component parts. The first sub-target behavior would be to walk around the block in ten minutes, let's say. When you have achieved that objective, the amount of time can be reduced where you can now jog around the block in, say, six minutes. Gradually the length of the jogging and the speed of the jogging are increased until you can, in fact, negotiate a half-marathon—13.1 miles. Dividing complex behaviors into their component parts, Behaviorists call "Approximations to Behavior."

In my first book, *Who's Raising Whom?,* I give the example of a parent asking that a seven-year-old child learn to make his bed. To expect a child of that age to make his bed properly immediately, with perfectly tucked-in corners, is unreasonable. First, the child might be expected to simply tuck in his sheet and blankets and lay a bedspread over it. Next, the child might learn to move the bedspread around more appropriately. Finally, the child could ultimately learn how to make his or her bed in a completely satisfactory manner.

Theory of Education

Educationally, I believe that an effective teacher appropriately sequences the material. Most students fail—become "stuck"—because they "don't get" how the instructor got from A to B. In most cases the learner has the requisite knowledge or intelligence to process the information; the learner simply cannot comprehend how to get from step A to step B. Often the student quits in frustration. Sometimes so does the teacher. If the teacher can demonstrate the intermediate steps—A1-A2-A3, then B—the student will learn the new information. Thus, breaking the task into its component parts—"Approximations to Behavior"—is the Behavioral theory of education. I call it "Precision Teaching."

A Treatment for Anxiety

This notion of breaking Target Behaviors into their component parts is also often used by Behavioral therapists to treat phobias. For example, I work with several personal injury attorneys who refer individuals to me who have been in car wrecks. Many of these unfortunate persons are struggling with anxiety and have become phobic about driving. Some of these clients have not gotten behind the wheel since the fateful accident.

Using a technique known as "Systematic Desensitization," more commonly referred to as "Baby Steps," I first have the client sit in the driver's seat of his or her car parked in their driveway with the ignition off for five to ten minutes (often while practicing stress management exercises), three to four times per week. (This is often the first time this person has been behind the wheel since the accident.) The next week or session I have the client start the engine, and "only if he or she is comfortable," put the car in gear and **only** go back and forth in the driveway. The following session I prescribe that the client, "only if he or she is comfortable," back the car out of the driveway and drive back and forth on their own street (assuming it is not a freeway). The driving requirement gradually becomes more intense until the client is comfortably driving as before—or close to that. This concept is obviously based on the Behavioral notion of Approximations to Behavior and the idea that you cannot fear something to which you are gradually and frequently exposed.

Step 4 in Behavior Modification:
Intervention

Once you identify the Target Behavior and conduct the baseline, the next step is to implement an intervention. The three intervention choices, which can be used in combination, are the three consequences to behavior (which were outlined previously)—reinforcement, extinction, and punishment.

Reinforcement

By far, reinforcement is the most preferred intervention because it is the most pleasant and the most effective. Decades of research confirms that it is far easier to change an undesirable behavior by reinforcing the alternative desired behavior than punishing the undesired behavior. Frequently, when parents ask me what I recommend they do when their child misbehaves (implying a punishment consequence), I typically ask them, "What would you prefer your child do instead?" When they provide an answer, I then say, "Reinforce that!"

When a toddler crawls toward a plant and is about to make a mess, for example, the parent can yell at the child or choose to distract the child toward something equally interesting, but safer and cleaner. When the kids squabble in the backseat of the car, the parent can scream at them to stop, or invite them to play "Who can be the first to find the next five yellow cars?"

When your spouse only rarely does something you would like to see more often, you could complain loudly, or choose to reinforce that when he or she exhibits the preferred behavior.

Despite the proven efficacy of reinforcing the alternative desired behavior, as seen in the above examples, most people persist in punishing the undesired action.

Reinforcement is defined as the application of something rewarding following a particular appropriate behavior which should increase the likelihood of that behavior. For children, reinforcement generally takes the form of contingent parental time—verbal praise, quality time, or maybe a hug. Reinforcement is not money or candy. For adults, reinforcement can be the same as with children, but could include money.

For reinforcement to be effective, two rules must be followed: The reinforcement must be **specific** and **immediate**. The objective of reinforcement is to **reward** the individual for exhibiting a desired behavior and **educate** that individual how to behave in a similar situation. The receiver of the reinforcement, then, must clearly and specifically understand why they earned the reinforcement.

Some Examples

"Jacob, I really like the way you cooperatively played that board game with your sister, by taking turns with her, speaking softly to her and not yelling at or pushing her. Let's make brownies together for dessert tonight."

"Susie, I loved it when you immediately went up to your room and cleaned it, as we defined, the first time I asked you to do so. Let's sit on the couch and have you read a book to me."

"Dear, I very much appreciate it when you remember to leave the garage light on for me when I come home in the dark. It makes me feel more comfortable and tells me you are thinking of me. Thank you."

"When I lose five pounds from eating according to my new diet and exercising per my new plan, I will treat myself to buy a new workout outfit."

Over my career I have seem many behavioral programs fail because the reinforcement was not immediate—too delayed—or was victimized by the dreaded "in a row" notion. For example, to contract with a child that he/she must behave in a certain manner "for a week," is very likely to be unsuccessful. While a week feels like a reasonable "bite-sized" chunk of time for an adult, to a child it is an eternity. To ask children to regulate their behavior on Monday so they can earn a reward on Saturday, simply will not work. The reward is too far off. (This would be akin to asking adults to save money every month so that they will ultimately have a nice retirement.) For children (and most adults) the reinforcement must be more immediate.

If an overweight adult tonight ate a very reasonable dinner and then immediately upon finishing the meal stepped on a scale and saw that he had lost two pounds, how difficult would it be to continue eating in that manner?

Obviously, continuing to eat appropriately would be relatively easy because of the great power of immediate reinforcement. Unfortunately, in many things—like eating or saving money—the immediate reinforcement of the good taste of the fatty food or the enjoyment of the purchase, overcomes the long-term reward of eating healthfully or saving for the future.

The problem with the "in a row" notion was evidenced recently when working with a young couple who had a six-year-old boy, Jimmy, who had a bedwetting issue. Jimmy had never been dry overnight for two mornings consecutively in his young life. Mother and Father had done some reading and came upon the idea of establishing a "token economy" behavioral program for Jimmy. They told Jimmy that if he woke up dry "every morning for a week," they would buy him the new bike he wanted. They even gave Jimmy a picture of the bike they would purchase. Jimmy was excited about the program and said he would try.

Jimmy went four mornings dry following the implementation of the program but, unfortunately, awoke wet on the fifth morning. The parents' response was to express disappointment and recommend another "week's" program. Jimmy's reaction was to tear up the picture of the bicycle and walk out of the room.

Jimmy had never been dry two mornings consecutively in his life and the new program incented him to go four mornings dry, which was a huge step for him. Nevertheless, Jimmy's "payoff" was parental disappointment, no bike, and another "week" of programming—at which he likely would fail again. Clearly, these parents needed a course in the power of immediate reinforcement.

I recommended to these parents that if Jimmy awakens dry, he should be loudly praised and a colorful sticker should be placed on a piece of paper, entitled "Jimmy's Bike Chart." When Jimmy earns seven stickers—not necessarily "in a row"—he gets his bike. Jimmy "earned" his bike in ten days. He and his parents were happy and proud. Moreover, Jimmy's bedwetting was essentially "cured" after that, as Jimmy learned he could control his behavior.

Human behavior is never perfect. The goal of Behavior Modification is to induce better behavior, not necessarily perfect behavior. Relapses are common. If you "fall off the wagon, get back on."

Punishment

Punishment is defined as the converse of reinforcement: Something unrewarding that decreases the likelihood of a particular, inappropriate behavior. Like reinforcement, punishment involves the same two rules as reinforcement—being specific and immediate. The person being punished must know exactly what behavior is being punished. Telling teens, for example, they are grounded because of their "bad attitude," is a misuse of punishment because the teens are unaware of what they did wrong and, importantly, what they should do instead. As with reinforcement, the recipient of the punishment must have a clear understanding of what the misbehavior "looked like" and what they should do instead.

For example:

"Billy, you know the rule is no eating outside the kitchen, yet you chose to bring food into your room. I am disappointed in your behavior. Your consequence is "no electronics" for the remainder of the day."

Punishment should be immediate, short-term, and administered calmly, as seen above. My favorite story regarding the misapplication of punishment recently occurred:

Jason's Mother punished him by "removing electronics" (a popular consequence nowadays) "for a week."

A few days later Jason asked Mother if he could watch TV.

Mother replied, "No, you are restricted from all electronics, including TV, until Friday." (It was Wednesday.)

Jason responded, "But why?"

Mother answered, "I don't recall right now but I know you can't watch TV till Friday."

If the purpose of punishment is to reduce a particular inappropriate behavior, what is the value of the punishment if neither the punisher nor the punishee can recall what the misbehavior was?

Punishment with children might involve "Time-Out" (being sent to the room) for as many minutes long (being quiet) as they are years old. Time-Out is appropriately used until age 8 or 9. For older children and teens "Response-Cost" (loss of electronics for the day) or being "grounded" for the day are more age-appropriate. A brief assertive comment regarding the undesired behavior is best when dealing with a teen or an adult:

"When you said/did _____, I felt _____;
I would like you to say/do _____ instead.""

You can choose to punish yourself: Last year while working with someone who was committed to quitting smoking, part of his intervention was if he cheated, an envelope with cash in it was automatically mailed to a very much disliked political organization.

Punishment should always be paired with reinforcement. Punishment should never be used as the sole intervention to change behavior—but parents, spouses, and managers continue to do so. Research finds that with the sole use of punishment the residual effect is not a change in the misbehavior but a change in the punishee becoming more conscious of the punisher. When motorists receive a speeding ticket, for example, they drive slower for the next 2-3 days, but they then resume their speeding. Weeks later they are still speeding—but they have become much more vigilant about police cars.

How many employees work in an environment where good behavior is ignored (Extinguished) but any problem results in an immediate visit with the manager (Punishment)? How do employees feel about working in such a place? How loyal does this management style make them feel? How likely is it that a worker in this situation will attempt to be creative or innovative and risk creating a problem?

What typically occurs with this style of management is that most employees do just enough to "stay under the radar." Ironically, while most employees hate this form of management, they come home and parent their children or treat their partner in the very same manner.

Extinction

Extinction is the process of causing a behavior to drop out— "become extinct"—by not reinforcing it. Essentially, extinction is "planned ignoring." For nearly four decades I have had parents become surprised but very impressed with the power of extinction, by essentially doing nothing.

I love to prescribe this "experiment" to parents:

"The next time your kids start arguing or fighting, simply get up, without saying a word, walk into your bedroom, leave the door open, sit on your bed, and wait."

When I say this most parents respond with something like, "There'll be blood on the floor if I leave them fighting! They will injure each other!"

What parents, in fact learn, is that within 30 seconds the kids find their parents and bring the fight to them:

"He started it!"

"She won't share!"

"He's mean!"

What this experiment quickly teaches is that, for the most part, kids fight because they have learned that such behavior elicits a response from their parent(s). Once parents recognize they do not have to "play referee" every time their kids decide to argue and understand that their kids will not maim each other, the parent can simply choose to ignore it. Extinction will probably not ever completely eradicate siblings fighting, but it will significantly reduce the conflict.

Choosing to ignore a particular problematic behavior in someone—child, partner, boss—rather than reacting to it, can be an effective intervention. Obviously, extinction will not apply if someone is attempting to modify his or her own behavior. Often, a combination of reinforcement of the new desired behavior and extinction of the undesired behavior can be a very powerful intervention.

If someone has been reinforced for a particular behavior for a time, and suddenly the reinforcement stops what is likely to happen? What happens is that for a brief time the original behavior increases, perhaps out of frustration, but then it begins to decline. This phenomenon is called an "extinction effect." Therefore, if you choose to ignore some behavior as part of a program you must be prepared to accept a brief initial increase in the behavior before it declines. For example, ignoring the children arguing, for a bit, but then responding to the children when their fighting becomes worse, will teach them they have to argue more vigorously to get your attention. Parents have been trapped by this "extinction effect" since Columbus discovered the New World.

To complete this step in behavior modification you must decide on what intervention(s) to use—reinforcement, reinforcement and extinction, reinforcement and punishment, or reinforcement, extinction, and punishment. You will also have to determine the schedule on how these interventions are to be applied. Generally, most interventions will primarily use reinforcement. The typical schedule of reinforcement is initially to reinforce the desired behavior continually. As the new and improved behavior becomes more developed, the reinforcement should be gradually attenuated to a more intermittent schedule.

If you are also using extinction with the reinforcement, the extinction of the inappropriate behavior should be used on a continuous basis. Obviously, you would not use extinction when modifying your own behavior because you cannot ignore yourself.

If you choose to use punishment as part of your intervention, the punishment, like extinction, should always be used on a continuous basis. Punishment also can be used if attempting to change your own behavior as noted above.

Step 5 in Behavior Modification:
Implement the Intervention(s)

Once the target behavior has been identified and baselined, the intervention(s) has/have been determined, and the schedule of reinforcement has been chosen, it is time to implement the program. After the program is implemented the target behavior must regularly be monitored.

Step 6 in Behavior Modification:
Evaluation and Adjustment

The final step in the process of behavior modification is to evaluate the progress of the target behavior and adjust it as necessary. If satisfactory progress is being made, the schedule of reinforcement should be maintained. Over time, the reinforcement schedule, as noted previously, can be faded to a more intermittent level. If the new behavior regresses with the fading of the reinforcement, the original reinforcement schedule may have to be re-implemented.

If the target behavior has not changed much, a few adjustments should also be considered: The target behavior may have to be divided into a simpler, more achievable behavior (approximation). The reward value of the reinforcement might have to be increased or extinction and/or punishment, if not already used, might have to be introduced.

Generally speaking, if the new target behavior is in evidence for approximately ninety days, it is likely to become a new positive ingrained pattern. Once your new target behavior is ingrained, you can think about the next new behavior you may want to develop.

By understanding and appropriately implementing the principles of behavior psychology, you will be able to change your behavior or the behavior of others in an effective, positive manner. In this fashion you will be able to move forward and achieve your life objectives.

Important Points to Remember in Chapter Six

1. Don't wait to **feel** like, or **get around to** doing what you should. Do it!

2. Don't "do depression."

3. Behave "as if." Remember, it is far easier to **behave** your way into a new **feeling** than **feel** you way into a new **behavior**.

4. The Behavior school views mental health as learning and exhibiting positive, adaptive behaviors; mental illness is the result of learning and exhibiting negative, maladaptive behaviors; and treatment is changing those inappropriate behaviors through the process of **behavior modification**.

5. Behavior modification consists of 5 steps: Identify the **Target Behavior**; **Baseline** it; if necessary, divide the Target Behavior into its component behaviors (**approximations**); identify the interventions of **Reinforcement** and/or **Extinction** and/or **Punishment** and the schedule of Reinforcement; implement the program and monitor the Target Behavior; and evaluate the program and change as needed.

6. Reinforcing the desired behavior is more effective than punishing the undesired behavior.

7. Identifying a Target Behavior, Baselining, Approximations, and Reinforcement comprise the cornerstone of Behavior Therapy.

CHAPTER SEVEN

Common Expressions to Explain Behavior According to The Four Schools of Psychological Thought

We often use expressions or idioms in casual conversation to explain human behavior. Most people fail to appreciate that these sayings are based on one of the four schools of psychology.

The following expressions can be categorized according to the **Biological** view:

"He/she is the black sheep of the family."

"He/she is a chip off the old block."

"The apple does not fall far from the tree."

"He/she has a screw loose."

"Blood is thicker than water."

"He/she is cut from the same cloth."

The following expressions can be categorized according to the **Analytic/Freudian** view:

"He/she was born with a silver spoon in his/her mouth."

"He has a chip on his shoulder."

"He is tied to his mother's apron strings."

The following expression can be categorized according to the **Cognitive** view:

> "I'll believe it when I see it."

The following expressions can be categorized according to the **Behavioral** view:

> "Monkey see monkey do."

> "It takes two to tango."

> "Birds of a feather flock together."

> "He's wet behind his ears."

CHAPTER EIGHT

Life Goals

"Your income is the average of your ten best friends."

Robert Allen

Life goals—dreams—are good. We all should have at least one, probably more. Goals and dreams give us direction and hope. I often ask clients to speak of their goals, dreams and hopes and, if necessary, help them to better define them. I then suggest that they try to live each day—or at least each week—such that they take a step closer to their goal. I often ask:

"Is how you are thinking and/or behaving taking you closer or further away from your goal(s)?

"Are you still baking cake or are you beginning to make a pie?"

Financial Independence

In the research to write this book I read many works on attaining financial freedom. Four books in particular, I believe, are classics in this field:

Think and Grow Rich by Napoleon Hill
The Richest Man in Babylon by George S. Clason
Rich Dad Poor Dad by Robert Kiyosaki, and
Secrets Of The Millionaire Mind: Mastering the Inner Game of Wealth by T. Harv Eker.

Hill's book unquestionably is the "granddaddy" of the financial wellness genre. Frankly, it is mind-blowing to recognize that it was written in the 1930's. The book is just as valid and relevant today, despite being published nearly 80 years ago.

Hill referred to "Thirteen Principles of Success." Some of his ideas that resonated with me were as follows:

His one Biological notion was:
"The brain is a broadcasting and receiving station for thought."

His one Analytic idea was:
"Man has the power to influence his own subconscious mind—autosuggestions for the maintenance of the principles of success"

Hill was a fan of Cognitive psychology:
"All achievement and success had their beginning in an idea."
"Man needs desire—and faith."
"If you think you are beaten, you are."
"There are no limitations to the mind except those we acknowledge."
"Professors often have little money. Henry Ford (a contemporary of Hill) had little education but was very rich."
"Success requires no explanation; failure permits no alibis."
"Failure leads to success."

His Behavioral tips were:
"Set clear, defined goals."
"Have a purpose and do not be stopped by temporary setbacks."
"Be prepared. There is a difference between wishing for success and being ready for it."

The Richest Man in Babylon was written around the same time as Hill's work. It didn't become quite as popular as Hill's book, but it has stood the test of time. It is simply written as an allegory about a wise man in biblical times. This book should be required reading for every high school student.

Below are concepts espoused by Clason that follow the Behavioral Model:

"A fat purse empties if there are no golden streams to fill it" (Today this is referred to as having several sources of passive income streams.)

"Part of all I earn is mine to keep."

"Every gold piece you save is a slave to work for you."

"For each ten coins I earn, I spend but nine."

"Wealth is like a tree. It grows from a tiny seed. The sooner you plant that seed the sooner shall the tree grow. The more faithful you nourish that tree with constant saving, the sooner you may bask in contentment beneath its shade."

"Learn to seek advice from men who are wiser than you." (I guess there were no wise women then.)

"Control by expenditures. That which we call 'necessary expenditures' will always grow equal to our incomes, unless we protest to the contrary."

"Guard thy treasure by investing only where the principal is safe. Better a little caution than a great regret."

"Take advantage of opportunity. Men of action are rewarded by the Goddess of Good Luck."

"We cannot afford to be without adequate protection." (Insurance companies love this one.)

"Where the determination is, the way can be found."

"Study and become wiser in the ways of money."

The only cognitive notion Clason purported was:

"Acquire the confidence to achieve your desires."

Kiyosaki's book, *Rich Dad, Poor Dad,* came out in 2000 and was a huge success. His work provides excellent Cognitive and Behavioral ideas.

His top Cognitively-based tips are:

"The lack of money is the root of all evil." (Originally a quote attributed to Mark Twain)

"Do not think I cannot afford it; think how I can afford it."

"Don't work for money; have your money work for you."

"Learn to use your emotions to think, not think with your emotions."

"Broke is temporary; poor is eternal."

"Self-doubt and fear, primarily, keep most people poor."

Kiyosaki's top Behaviorally-based tips are:

"Get educated regarding money."

"Don't be book smart but financially illiterate."

"Read, take courses, attend seminars."

"Use smart financial consultants."

"Study hard; get good grades; and find a good company to buy."

"Start a business. Few people become financially independent by working for someone else."

"The poor only have expenses; the middle class buy liabilities; and the rich buy assets."

"Pay yourself first."

"Learn good money management habits."

"Wealth is not how much you earn but how much you keep."

"Associate with people who are wealthy."

Eker's Secrets of the Millionaire Mind: Mastering the Inner Game of Wealth, published in 2005, was instantly a best seller, and is, by far, the most psychological of the four books. Eker writes about "Wealth Files" which detail how rich people think and act differently than the non-rich. Eker and his company, Peak Potentials, offer intense workshops regarding money and money-related topics. I participated in two of these workshops and recommend them highly. His tips for becoming successful cover all the schools of psychological thought.

Eker provides one tip from the Biological Perspective:

"The rich believe 'I create my life.' The poor believe 'Life happens to me.'"

The following tips adhere to the Analytic view:

"If you want to change the fruits of the tree, you first have to change the roots."

"There are four elements of change: Awareness, understanding, dissociation, and reconditioning." (This is quite similar to how I recommended people grow from the Analytic view.)

"The goal is to live from true choices in the present rather than be run by programming from the past." (Again, not to live by faulty Truths.)

The following tips come from the Cognitive school:

"Thoughts lead to feelings. Feelings lead to actions. Actions lead to results." (Pure Cognitive theory)

"Consider only those thoughts and feelings that empower you."

"Rich people manage money to win. Poor people manage money to not lose."

"The rich focus on opportunities. The poor focus on obstacles."

"The rich value and promote themselves. The poor think negatively regarding selling and promotion."

"The rich act in spite of fear. The poor let fear stop them."

Finally, the following tips are based on the Behavioral point of view:

"People don't get what they want because they don't know what they want." (Amorphous, undefined goals)

"Ready, fire, aim." (Don't wait for things to be perfect; act and adjust—one of the steps of Behavior Modification.)

"How you do anything is how you do everything."

"The rich get paid on results. The poor get paid based on time."

"If you are willing to do only what's easy, life will be hard. But if you're willing to do what's hard, life will be easy." (Remember my discussion with Josh that I was glad his college business classes were "hard.")

Waldman's Financial Tips

Educate yourself! Read about finances and investing. (Perhaps you could begin with the books in this bibliography.) Attend seminars.

Consult a financial planner. A good consultant will help you with a budget and establish a long-term plan, not just try to sell you life insurance.

It's not how much you make but how much you keep. (Someone who manages their money well over time will do far better than someone who earns a larger income but mismanages their funds.)

Develop and adhere to a budget.

Save money specifically to invest.

Pay yourself first. (AFTER you put your saved investment money aside)

Think long term. Money regularly saved each month or paycheck over time will become substantial. Each dollar put away for retirement or investment when 30 years old could be worth $50.00 or more when age 65.

Keep thinking of entrepreneurial concepts and opportunities. A good idea could be worth a million dollars.

Think about starting a side Internet business.

If you can't afford it, don't buy it. If you truly need it, save for it.

The only things you should finance, I believe, are your house and your car.

When financing your house and/or car try to pay an additional $100.00 per month toward the mortgage and, if you can, put an additional $50.00 per month on the car payment. This is money well spent. Depending on the cost of your house, of course, doing this over a 30-year mortgage would probably cut four to five years or so off the payments—or you will have more equity when you sell it. (This tip applies, of course, if your house is not "under water.")

Use your credit card and enjoy its convenience but pay the bill in full every month. If you can't pay the monthly bill, stop using it until you can.

Do your utmost to fund, to the maximum, your employer's 401K program and/or your Roth IRA, or your SEP IRA if self-employed, if at all possible. It is essentially free money.

If you don't have enough income to regularly invest, try to accrue that income by cutting back on some expenses. If necessary, consider developing a side business or taking on a part-time job for investment income only. It's not so bad working another job if you know that money will soon be working for you.

Don't ignore your creditors. Contact your creditor(s) and work out a payment plan. Don't do nothing and end up in collections.

Associate with wealthy friends or, at least, people who have forward-thinking ideas.

Lifestyle

The data are clear. The number one killer of adults in the USA is **lifestyle**. Too many of us still **smoke**, consume **alcohol** too much and too often, **eat poorly**, and get **insufficient exercise**. Life sometimes plays a cruel joke, I believe. When we are young and healthy we don't have the time or the money to do the things we would like to do. When we become older we have the time and hopefully the money to do the things we would like to do but we don't have the health to do them. What is the sense of working toward financial independence or your other life goals if you aren't going to be around or be healthy enough to enjoy them?

Smoking

Smoking is the deadliest of the lifestyle sins. Current statistics indicate a long-term smoker will likely die about ten years earlier than if he or she had not smoked. What the data does not indicate, though, is that the ten to 15 years before death are also far from optimal.

If you are smoking I recommend that you contact the American Cancer Society and quickly get into a smoking cessation program.

Most of these programs are based on Behavioral psychology. Put aside the money previously used for cigarettes (about five to six dollars a pack, today) and use that money as reinforcement. I have had a number of clients loudly complain regarding medication that cost them one to three dollars per day but have no problems spending six dollars a day for their nicotine. Do yourself and your family a huge favor and quit.

Alcohol

Do you drink nearly daily and more on weekends?

Has your partner or other family member recently complained about your alcohol intake?

Have you gotten into a fight or into a compromising situation due to alcohol?

Do you and your partner have the biggest arguments when you are drinking?

Have you had a DUI?

Have you missed work due to alcohol or gone to work with a hangover?

Have you ever been drinking and cannot remember what occurred during that drinking episode?

Do you have a direct relative—parent, grandparent, or sibling—who has a confirmed problem with alcohol?

If you answered yes to any of the above questions and to the last question you may well have a problem with alcohol. If you have an issue with alcohol, I suggest you contact a mental health provider who is experienced in dealing with drugs and/or alcohol. This professional will advise you regarding your alcohol concern. Attending AA meetings certainly would be beneficial—and they are free. Most alcohol programs today are conducted on an out-patient basis—three evenings per week, three or four hours per evening. The 28-day stay in a facility has essentially gone away.

Proper Eating

Become educated regarding proper, nutritious eating. Go online or check with your physician's office for recommended eating plans put out by the Diabetic or Heart Associations, for example:

Consult a nutritionist.

Develop a meal plan for every week.

Grocery shop according to your meal plan. Avoid buying "junk."

An alcoholic should not have beer in the fridge. An overweight person should not have bags of cookies and candies in the pantry. If you don't buy it, you can't eat it.

Recognize that what you eat at each meal is a **choice**. Will you choose a fatty, starchy, surgery meal or a nutritious one? By continuing to make the right choice over time your body (and pants belt) will thank you.

Pack your own lunch. In this manner you get to choose your food rather than have to select it from the menu. Your lunch, then, will likely be more nutritious, less fattening, and a whole lot cheaper. My lunch typically consists of a piece of chicken taken from a whole chicken that I buy each week, a small cup of low fat yogurt, a fruit, and a water bottle filled with good quality water.

Snack on fruit and veggies—cut up celery or carrot sticks.

Watch portion control. Put a reasonable portion of food on your plate and put the rest of the food in the fridge. You do not have to consume everything on your plate or in the pot in one meal. In a restaurant, ask the waiter for a doggie bag as soon as your food arrives. Put one-half of your meal immediately into the bag and have that for lunch or dinner the following day.

If dessert is served have a bite or two of it. Don't deprive yourself. However, after a bite or two put pepper on the rest of it so you are not tempted to finish it.

Generally speaking, the average sedentary male requires about 2,000 calories a day to maintain his weight and the average female requires about 1,600 calories to maintain her weight.

Approximately 3,500 calories equal a pound of body weight. Therefore, if you consume fewer calories than your standard caloric requirement per day you will gradually lose weight. On the other hand, if you consume more than 2,000 or 1,600 calories per day, depending on your gender, you will gain weight. Thus, if you consume 500 calories less per day than your standard over the course of the week you will lose approximately a pound. On the other hand, unfortunately, if you consume 500 calories more than your standard requirements every day for a week, you will gain around a pound.

You can influence this formula by adding exercise to the equation. By exercising more you burn more calories. So if you eat the same number of calories as before and add exercise to your daily routine, you will begin to lose weight fairly quickly.

According to many treadmills that I have been on, I know that if I run two miles in 20 minutes I will burn approximately 225 to 250 calories. If you take a stroll around the block for 20 minutes, depending on your fitness level, you will probably burn in the neighborhood of 50 calories. It is difficult to burn 500 calories per day, unless you are a long distance runner. Nevertheless, by continuing to eat somewhat less than your standard requirement and increase your exercise, very quickly you will begin to notice that your pants fit better and you will also feel the health benefits of the exercise.

When I look at a two-inch-square fudge brownie and recognize that it has approximately 250 to 300 calories in it and it would take me 20 minutes of hard running to balance those calories out, you can understand why I often choose to eat a piece of fruit instead.

You know by now that I like to keep things simple. The simple process of consuming fewer calories and exercising more is the best long-term approach to weight control. Fad diets are a waste of time, energy and money. The research clearly indicates that such plans cause brief weight loss but once they stop the weight comes back—plus.

In summary, make a weekly meal plan (just like a budget to manage your money). Grocery shop according to that plan (it will be healthier and probably cheaper). Choose your meals (not eat impulsively or give in to the desire for sugar or fat). Watch your portions (try eating off of smaller plates). Snack on fruits and veggies. And exercise.

Exercise and Conditioning

If you are about to start an exercise/conditioning program, consult with your physician to ensure you are healthy enough to do so. Once you receive the green light, I suggest you connect with a gym and consult with a trainer for a time to learn and develop a basic exercise program and understand how to use the equipment correctly. I like the gym because it is a place you go and the time can be scheduled. While home equipment is nice and convenient, it is my experience, and also many clients tell me, it is easy to fall into the "I'll get around to it" syndrome. Your workouts should be scheduled—either at home or in the gym. I say this often:

"Don't schedule your workouts around your life; schedule your life around your workouts, because workouts extend and improve your life."

Conditioning consists of three components:

aerobic fitness,

strength/stamina,

and flexibility.

Therefore, workouts should consist of some aerobic exercise— running, jogging, walking on the treadmill or the pavement, biking on the road or on a stationary bike, or using one of the various machines at the gym—such as the cross-country skier, or stair-stepper. You could also jump rope, roller skate, or boxercize.

For best results the aerobic exercise should be done at least three times a week for 20 minutes in the "training zone." The training zone is defined as 80% of one's standard heart rate capacity at a particular age. I recommend doing an Internet search on "training zone" and find the proper training zone per your age. Many aerobic machines will monitor your heart rate or you can buy a simple heart rate monitor.

Every workout should include ten to 20 minutes of stretching. Check online for a recommended set of full body stretches. Stretching probably should be done before the aerobic exercise. I recommend stretching and doing your aerobic workout before your strength training, especially as you get older, because it is important to stretch and warm up your muscles. If your trainer, on the other hand, recommends doing your aerobic work after your strength training then you can follow that order.

Strength training or weight training (commonly called weight lifting), should be done twice per week for most people. Strength training strengthens and tones muscles and associated tendons and ligaments. It also helps build bone density, which is extremely important as we age. Women should also do strength training. Don't worry about becoming big and bulky.

Body builders train five to six times per week and will work on different body parts every other day or so. For most people, though, a full body workout—involving legs, back, chest, shoulders, and arms—twice per week will be sufficient. Abs can and should be done every workout—three times per week.

Training and conditioning need to be done consistently. If you do it just once a week all you are essentially doing is making yourself sore. Very little improvement will come from that schedule.

In weight training I do an exercise, say an arm bicep curl, 15 times ("reps" for repetitions) with excellent form; when I can do 20 reps with good form I increase the weight. I do three "sets" of each exercise—15 reps three times, resting 60-90 seconds between each set. I do most exercises single-handed or single-footed so to not over-train my right (dominant) side.

It doesn't matter where you are with respect to your physical condition when you start an exercise program. Everybody has to start somewhere. You may have to begin with walking on the treadmill for five minutes at two miles per hour and begin lifting two pound weights. Great! That's a start. You will be amazed at how quickly your body will adapt and grow stronger with proper consistent training. In fact, the greatest gains are seen early on.

Relationships

Personal Growth

The primary relationship is the one you have with yourself. The previous chapters discuss making personal changes to grow, mature, become more mindful, and become more accepting and tolerant. Please review those chapters.

Educate yourself. Read books (again, peruse the attached bibliography), attend seminars.

Join a support group.

See a therapist.

Check around to find an experienced clinician. Don't select your personal therapist like a plumber—the one who is the closest, available, or cheapest will do. Ask your friends if they have seen or know of an excellent therapist. If you cannot find or afford a selected (cash-pay) clinician, you can use your health insurance. Sometimes the mental health practitioner you find on your own also happens to be in your insurance provider network. When you use your insurance, you will have to pay any deductible and co-pays according to your policy. (As with any use of your healthcare insurance, it is recorded.) If you do not have insurance and/or cannot afford the insurance co-pay, you can get counseling at a community mental health center, where the cost is minimal.

Improve Your Relationship with Your Significant Other and/or Your Children

Again, become educated. There are several excellent books (like mine) on enhancing your marriage and strengthening the parent-child relationship.

Join a couples group and/or parenting group.

Again, seek a therapist. Ensure that the professional has considerable experience with marital treatment and/or parenting.

See the discussion on finding a mental health provider above.

Make a point of regularly acknowledging positive behavior in your partner and/or your child.

Write That Book

At least once per week when a client sees my book covers on my office wall they say, "I wish I could write a book, novel, or autobiography."

I always answer, "Then do it!"

Many of us have led interesting lives, have something to say, or have great imaginations. Nan's best friend, in her late 60's, is in the process of writing her first novel. Nan has read the first draft of the manuscript and said the sex scenes are great. (Maybe she'll learn something?)

Not long ago I was talking to a gentleman I occasionally see at the gym. He told me he has an elderly relative (grandfather or uncle, I forget) who survived the Bataan Death March and lived in the Filipino jungle for several years and joined a band of guerilla fighters against the Japanese. He didn't learn the war was over for months after the truce. I said to this guy that he should record his relative telling the story and write a book about it. It would be fascinating, I thought.

To write a book, first develop a general outline.

Everyday, if at all possible, write at least a page or two. Don't concern yourself with editing or proper punctuation. Just get the words out. If you don't type, write it long-hand or record it orally. Check online for a service in which you can dictate over the phone and the service will transcribe your words into a word document.

Once you have some printed pages, you can begin the editing process. Give the manuscript to your family members, relatives, other relatives, and friends to read to get their comments, suggestions, and corrections.

Some people are satisfied with the completed manuscript. If you are one of them, fine. If someone wants to read your manuscript, you can print one out for them.

If you are not one of the above and want more people to read what you wrote, you will have to get your book published. You can try to have your book managed by a publishing house or you can self-publish.

To have your work published by a publishing house, you will probably need a literary agent. Most publishers will not review unsolicited manuscripts. You can find an agent by perusing books that are in the same field as your book, contact the publisher and ask to learn of the agent. You can also look up literary agents online that work with books of your genre. Contact the selected agent to discuss if he or she will represent your book.

If the agent agrees to represent you—and don't become upset if you are turned down—the agent will submit your manuscript to his or her publishing contacts. If the publisher decides to take on the project—and, again, don't be surprised if most don't—the agent will get a piece (usually around 15%) of everything you, the author, receive—a small advance and royalties (usually around 15% of the wholesale proceeds). If you are so fortunate to secure a publisher, be sure that the publisher not only will publish your work but will also promote it—through book tours, book signings, and media presentations.

If you choose to self-publish, the advantages are total content control and you receive all the profits when you make a sale. The disadvantages are that you have to edit the book, design the front and back covers, convert the book from manuscript to book form, deal with the copyright issues, find a printer, pay up front for the printing, and, most importantly, market the book once it's printed. You can market your book by arranging your own book tours and book signings. You can sell your book if you speak (as I do) and list it on Amazon. You can also arrange to have your book sold as an e-book.

Epilogue

My objective with this book is to help you achieve your life goals using accepted tenets of the four schools of psychology. If you have read this far, I hope you are on your way to attaining your dreams.

"Don't Wait For Your Ship to Come In. Swim Out to It."

Let me know of your successes.

Larry F. Waldman Ph.D., ABPP
LarryWaldmanPhD@cox.net

Contact Dr. Waldman

Dr. Waldman has previously written four books:

Who's Raising Whom? A Parent's Guide to Effective Child Discipline, 1987/2004.
This book teaches parents how to learn to use behavioral psychology to effectively manage and discipline their children.

Coping with Your Adolescent, 1994.
In this book Dr. Waldman assists parents to more effectively cope and communicate with their teen.

How Come I Love Him But Can't Live With Him? How to Make Your Marriage Work Better, 2002.
This book teaches couples why marriages fail, how to communicate more effectively, how to give to get, and how to fight fair.

The Graduate Course You Never Had: How to Develop, Manage and Market a Flourishing Mental Health Practice— With and Without Managed Care, 2010.
Dr. Waldman in this book instructs mental health providers how to conduct their practices as a business, how to effectively manage and market their practices, and how to secure alternative methods of income.

Professional Speaking

Over the past 25 years Dr. Waldman has conducted many keynote addresses, seminars, and workshops across the country. His comprehensive vita is available upon request. Dr. Waldman presents to corporations, mental health private practitioners, school psychologists, school counselors, school social workers, school districts, and parent organizations.

To corporations Dr. Waldman presents:

- ◆ "How We Got Stuck In Our Rut and How to Get Unstuck: Reaching Our Potential"

- ◆ "Solving Our Problems by Behaving 'As If': It's No Secret"

- ◆ "How to Raise a Responsible Child"

- ◆ "Make Your Marriage Work Better"

- ◆ "Manage Your Stress"

- ◆ "The Psychology of Problem Solving"

- ◆ "Behavioral Principals of Effective Management"

To mental health practitioner organizations, Dr. Waldman presents:

- ◆ "The Graduate Course You Never Had"

- ◆ "Teaching Parents to Parent"

- ◆ "Using Solution-Focused Therapy in Individual and Couples Work"

To school psychologists, school counselors, school social workers and school districts, Dr. Waldman presents:

- ◆ "Teaching Parents to Parent"

- ◆ "Managing the Difficult Child in the Classroom"

- ◆ "Making Your Marriage Work Better"

To parent organizations Dr. Waldman presents:

- ◆ "How to Raise a Responsible Child"

To contact Dr. Waldman regarding his books and/or professional speaking:

Email: LarryWaldmanPhD@cox.net

Phone: Office (602-996-8619)
Cell (602-418-8161)

Address: Paradise Valley Office Suites
Building E, Suite 100
11020 North Tatum Blvd
Phoenix, AZ 85028

Web Site: TopPhoenixPsychologist.com

Bibliography

Allen, J. *As a Man Thinketh*, Penguin Books, London, England, 2008.

Blanchard, K., Hutson, D., & Willis, E. *The One-Minute Entrepreneur*, Doubleday, New York, NY, 2007.

Blanchard, K. & Miller, M. *Great Leaders Grow*, Barrett-Kohler Publishers, San Francisco, 2012.

Clason, G.S. *The Richest Man In Babylon*, Penguin Putnam, New York, NY, 1926

Collins, J. & Porras, J.I. *Built to Last: Successful Habits of Visionary Companies*, Harper Collins, New York, NY, 1994.

Covey, S. *The Seven Habits of Highly Successful People*, Free Press, New York, NY, 2004.

Duhigg, C. *The Power of Habit: Why We Do What We Do in Life and Business*, Random House, New York, NY, 2012.

Eker, T.H. *Secrets of the Millionaire Mind: Mastering the Inner Game of Wealth*, Harper Business, New York, NY, 2005.

Ferriss, T. *The 4-Hour Work Week*, Crown Publishers, New York, NY, 2007.

Gitomer, J. *The Little Green Book On Getting Your Way*, FT Press, Upper Saddle River, NJ, 2007.

Gladwell, M. *Blink: The Power of Thinking without Thinking*, Back Bay Books, NY, 2005.

Godin, S. *Tribes: We Need You to Lead Us*, Penguin Books, London, England, 2008.

Hill, N. *Think and Grow Rich*, Tribeca Books, USA, 1937

Kiyosaki, R. *Rich Dad Poor Dad*, Time Warner, New York, NY, 1998.

Scott, D.M. *The New Rules of Marketing and PR*, John Wiley and Sons, Hoboken, NJ, 2009.

Stanley, T.J. & Danko, W.D. *The Millionaire Next Door: The Surprising Secrets of America's Wealthy*, Taylor Trade Publishing, Lanham, MD, 1996.

Waldman, L.F. *Who's Raising Whom? A Parent's Guide to Effective Child Discipline*, UCS Press, Phoenix, AZ, 1987, 2007.

Waldman, L.F. *Coping with Your Adolescent*, Hampton Roads, Norfolk, VA, 1994.

Waldman, L.F. *How Come I Love Him But Can't Live With Him? How to Make Your Marriage Work Better*, Minuteman Press, Milwaukee, WI, 2002.

Waldman, L.F. *The Graduate Course You Never Had: How to Develop, Manage, and Market a Flourishing Mental Health Practice—With and Without Managed Care*, UCS Press, Phoenix, AZ, 2010.

Wattles, W.D. & Powell, J.L. *The Science of Getting Rich*, Top of the Mountain Publishing, Pinellas Park, FL, 1990.

Weiner-Davis, M. *Divorce Busting: A Step-by-Step Approach to Making Your Marriage Loving Again*, Fireside Publishing, New York, NY, 1992

Publisher's Note

All five of Dr. Waldman's books are available in print and e-book editions. You may order print edition books direct from Dr. Waldman, or via the publisher's web site:

www.MarJimBooks.com

You may also special order print editions of *Who's Raising Whom?*, *The Graduate Course You Never Had*, and *Too Busy Earning a Living to Make Your Fortune?* from booksellers throughout Canada and the U.S. Just tell the bookseller that he or she may order the book for you via Ingram's Online Catalog. Your order will be fulfilled within a few days.

Dr. Waldman's books also are available in print editions from Amazon, and other Internet sellers.

E-book editions are available via Amazon Kindle, Apple iPad, Barnes & Noble, Kobo, Smashwords, and Sony.

You might find other good books that are of interest to you at the publisher's web site:

www.MarJimBooks.com

UCS PRESS

Small Press. Big Reading Value.

www.ingramcontent.com/pod-product-compliance
Lightning Source LLC
LaVergne TN
LVHW021459080426
835509LV00018B/2341

SEEING THROUGH
The Game of Life

SEEING THROUGH
The Game of Life

A Practical Guide to Spiritual Enlightenment

by Bodhi Daya

First published 2012

Copyright © 2012 by Bodhi Daya. All Right Reserved

Published by the Bodhi Daya Foundation
www.bodhidaya.com – Saratoga, California

Art and Design: Bodhi's wife, Patricia.
Light Editing: Nora Boxer – Berkeley, California

ISBN 978-0-615-66759-1

Through laughter and the good company
of my wife, Patricia, this book was born.
May we continue to grow together, always –
in gratitude, love, and joy . . .

CONTENTS

6

7

Introduction

Enlightenment: *en·light·en·ment – a revelation or deep insight into the meaning and purpose of all things; also called self-realization or awakening; often including mystical experiences such as seeing through the game of life; etc.*

~Bodhi Daya

Enlightenment is seeing through the game of life. It is a self-fulfilling prophecy that begins with an awakening to who you truly are, your authentic self – and continues through a journey of discovery that ultimately sets you free from any thought, story, or projection that has been keeping you from experiencing the true nature of your existence. It is seeing through the veil of illusions that seem to separate us from every aspect of our own lives, to look through the eyes of God in order to have and act upon a fresh vision of reality in a "brave new world" – one that is full of wisdom, compassion and grace.

When you awaken to your authentic self, you begin to perceive and experience who you truly are, and how you truly move in the world: not as a philosophy, but in the actual context of reality. Your own innate wisdom that knows the difference between the two awakens, and aspects of your true nature that previously remained hidden from you suddenly become revealed to you in a single, spontaneous moment.

There is a shift away from looking for answers outside of yourself as you begin to realize that your parents, mentors, teachers, and books cannot provide you with all of the wisdom and experience that you are searching for. It is a rite of passage from not only being a student of life but to also becoming your own teacher in life, for your authentic self has a way of moving in the world that is extremely unique, precious and rare – one that can be pointed to, but cannot be taught by another.

Along the path of awakening to your authentic self, many new and mystical experiences will occur, honing your skills and refining your sense of perception to support a new way of living in the world, enlightened living. You will gain mastery of your own emerging set of mystical tools, such as having prophetic vision and foresight, conversations with God or angels, energy healing, presence and resonance, and so much more.

It is important to be open and explorative, to approach every mystical experience from a place of honesty and integrity, and allow the many twists and turns to occur naturally. These experiences profoundly change the way we think about ourselves and life, and the way we choose to be in the world. If cultivated with wisdom, intent, and purpose they can be transformative and add to the richness of our lives, and when the myths around these experiences are dispelled, they become as common to being human as waking up in the morning and having a cup of coffee.

Enlightenment is seeing through the game of life – seeing through your own thoughts, stories, and projections about life. It is the end of believing in and moving with such things. The end of this game is the dawn of enlightenment, the beginning of enlightened living, that of being a person who knows their authentic self to be made in the image of God and who acts from a place of this awareness.

"The spiritual journey does not consist of arriving at a new destination where a person gains what he did not have, or becomes what he is not. It consists in the dissipation of one's own ignorance concerning one's self and life, and the gradual growth of that understanding which begins the spiritual awakening. The finding of God is a coming to one's self."

~Aldous Huxley

1

A Brave New World

Seeing through the game of life is, to borrow Aldous Huxley's phrase, to live in a "brave new world". It is seeing through the veil of illusions that seem to separate us from every aspect of life, and acting upon this new vision as it appears to us. We are all one in the eyes of God. There are no true contradictions or discrepancies. Enlightenment is seeing through the eyes of God and living as the image of God, in the physical world.

Enlightenment is, as the Bible says, "a new heaven and a new earth". Seeing life through the eyes of God, through the eyes of your authentic self, is a new heaven – *enlightenment*. Living as the image of God in the physical world, and acting upon the vision of your authentic self, is a new earth – *enlightened living*. Both are a reflection of the same inner and outer truth of your authentic self.

Having a relationship with God can be the most personal experience any human being is capable of, as we ultimately come to discover, because it is characteristic of the relationship to one's self and the rest of life. It is the only relationship in which whatever is given to it is returned one thousand times over. For every step we take towards God, the Beloved takes one thousand more towards us. To walk along this path in each and every moment is to walk the path of enlightened living.

Several years ago, I closed my eyes for the first time in a very, very long time and rested in meditation. I looked into the vast, unknown territory of my mind and was surprised to have the sense of God looking back at me. The more I focused on this inner awareness of God, the more I perceived that God was actually looking for me. It then occurred to me that I was also looking for God. Through this connection I felt an indescribable longing to always know and be one with God. Thus began my conscious relationship with God in this lifetime.

Being in relationship with God has given me the opportunity to know another aspect of myself: the authentic self. The authentic self is your higher self. It is called "the egoless self" in some traditions. It is the ancient presence of your own being, the resounding voice of your true self, that which has been aware of each and every moment of your existence from the very beginning.

The authentic self is a voice of reason. It is profoundly flavored with the residue of your past lives. Your authentic self is guiding your every move in perfect accordance with God's ultimate plan, creating lessons in your life that serve the purpose of waking you up to your true nature, and awakening your ability to see through the game of life in a "brave new world" of enlightenment.

∞ ⚴ ∞

Practice Idea: Automatic Writing

Automatic writing is a practice of spontaneous and involuntary writing that is used to access sources of our subconscious and spiritual wisdom. Neale Donald Walsch, known for his book "Conversations with God", is said to have used automatic writing to initiate and chronicle his dialogues with God and his authentic self.

If your heart is pure and your intentions are true, you will be able to use this technique to have two-way conversations with God, your higher self, enlightened beings, guides, angels, guardians, or the dearly departed . . . all of which are forms of God in different states of consciousness.

Find a quiet area where you can sit and relax comfortably, and where you will not be interrupted. Bring a pen and journal with you.

Start with today's date and the subject you would like guidance on. For example, *I wish to learn more about opening a two-way conversation with God*. If you choose to do automatic writing for guidance on some other area of interest, you can write a different statement that addresses what you wish to learn.

Take a minute to relax and ease your mind. Try focusing on your breath for sixty seconds. Focus all of your awareness on your breathing, until you feel yourself to be present and alert. Imagine an arc of white light running from the base of your spine down through the earth. Feel the energy from the earth resonate up though the base of your spine, throughout your body, and out through the top of your head, into the sky above you.

See a purple-white light descending from the sky and entering your body through the top of your head. Feel the resonance of this light as it moves down the center of your body, out of the base of your spine, and down through the earth. Do this energetic practice until you feel solidly anchored between the earth and sky.

Ask for the highest guidance possible to answer your questions. Start to write when you feel moved by whatever comes into your mind, or moves through your hand. Do so without stopping. Do not try to read, filter, or analyze the information that comes through you, even if you do not understand the information or it does not seem to line up with your intention. Simply write until your hand stops writing. Now read what you have written. Be prepared to be amazed.

"I learned the most important lesson of my life: that the extraordinary is not the birthright of a chosen privileged few, but of all people, even the humblest. That is my one certainty: We are all the manifestation Of the divinity of God."

~Paulo Coelho

2

The Authentic Self

The authentic self, your true self, is unique in every way imaginable, and life is the soul expression of your depth of knowing just how authentic you truly are. There is no need to imitate or to follow the example of another person's expression of enlightenment, because knowing your authentic self ultimately comes down to seeing who you truly are in the world, and knowing how you truly move in it. By simply being aware of your own authentic vision of enlightenment as it unfolds in each and every moment, the wisdom and clarity that is unique to you and you alone will arise naturally.

The more we know how something works, the better we can use it, and the less we know how it works . . . let's just say that our iPods might as well be used as paperweights. The authentic self has a way of discovering life, of being and moving with it that is so very precious and rare. Although you may or may not yet know who you truly are, or how to be your authentic self in the world, life is beckoning you to do so continuously, and to live so accordingly.

Imagine looking into outer space through the lens of a telescope: What do you see? What are you looking at? What are you looking for? Just noticing the general tendency to look for something, such as another planet or a star, places you at half-way along the journey to discovering your authentic self. The other half of the journey can be likened to knowing that the rest of outer space is made up of mostly nothing, empty space. Actually, it is made up of a whole lot of nothing.

When we apply this analogy towards realizing the authentic self, we add balance and wholeness to our own perspective, because we acknowledge not only what we see, but what we do not see as being an important aspect of our experience and vision. Seeing through the game of life is having this complete awareness, and learning to actualize it as a truth that exists in every life lesson, which allows us to act with wisdom and compassion toward ourselves and the rest of the world – for these qualities come from having a perspective that is undivided, in support of unity and wholeness.

Soul Expression

We spend so much time and energy trying to either follow in or escape from the footsteps of our parents and predecessors. We sometimes hope to live up to their expectations, and at other times we try to get as far away from them as possible. They have passed their life lessons and experiences on down to us as if to say, "So what can *you* do with this?" We tend to look up to or down upon these examples, and choose to either accept or reject their lessons, which is what directly contributes toward our own process of conditioning, through what is known as positive and negative reinforcement.

Positive and negative reinforcement will either maintain or increase the frequency of a conditioned behavior, by offering a reward for its occurrence, *positive*, or lack thereof, *negative*. A thought is also a conditioned behavior, and the reinforcement of a pattern of thoughts to maintain or strengthen our sense of self is referred to as egoic conditioning.

Almost every pattern of thought that we have is a product of egoic conditioning that increases or maintains our sense of self by weighing past experiences against those we are having in this very moment. It is a process that allows us to compare our sense of self against that of another person, which inevitably makes us feel isolated from each other; separated.

In spirituality, this process is what leads us to compare ourselves to examples of divinity or enlightenment such as Jesus, the Buddha, Gandhi, or Mother Teresa . . . and how can we expect ourselves to measure up to the examples of compassion that have been handed down to us by Mother Teresa, or those of peace that have been handed down to us by Ghandi? Personally, I have yet to find a lasting way to live by their examples of compassion and peace.

Every briefly successful attempt I have ever made to follow in the footsteps of someone that I believed to be enlightened or divine turned at some point, into another failed attempt to lead a spiritual life. I simply could not sustain compassion for others as I trust Mother Teresa did. I could not keep my mind still as I trust the Buddha did. These human beings were messengers, who handed down to us examples of wisdom, truth, compassion, and peace. They were extraordinary in their own authentic ways.

The lesson that I learned from my own failed attempts to follow in their footsteps is that we are all capable of being extraordinary in our own authentic ways as well. We all have our own soul expression that comes directly from the authentic self. Having this realization is like falling through a crack in the sidewalk – an immediate release from the long, hard walk along a conditioned path. It is a moment of freedom, and a true taste of the authentic self.

In these moments of freedom we realize that the authentic self is always present and aware. It is present when all hope is lost, and when all hope is found. It fully embraces our capacity to sometimes be completely narrow-minded, and at other times full of wisdom. It is patiently watching as we try to sustain a state of compassion or peace. It is not only present when we realize our own ability to be selfless and in harmony with life, but also when we wage war with others and within ourselves. The authentic self is present when we judge others, and also when we suffer at the hands of our own judgments.

The authentic self was never born and will not die. It does not go to sleep at night, nor does it wake up in the morning. It does not miss a single aspect of your experience as a human being. It is simply present and aware. This is what we come to know and understand the more we experience moments of freedom from our own conditioned paths. We realize that the very thing we are looking for is also looking for us, and when the two come together as one, we see just how unique in form and expression, we truly are. So uncover all that is here to be seen, and leave no stone unturned.

∞ ② ∞

Practice Idea: In Meditation

Find your authentic self through meditation. Your authentic self is always present and aware. This can be seen when we take a break from our daily routines and distractions, find a quiet place to sit down, and meditate.

Be sure to sit comfortably in any position. Relax your body. Close your eyes. Let your attention rest on the flow of your breath. Listen to your breath as you breathe in, and breathe out. Breathe in, and breathe out.

As you move into a quieter state of being, you will become increasingly aware of your thoughts. Simply allow your thoughts to come and go. There is no need to engage them. There is no need for contemplation. Keep your awareness on the flow of your breath. Breathe in, and breathe out.

It may be helpful to internally chant a mantra, such as repeating the sacred syllable AUM (pronounced "Om") or HU (pronounced "Hue"), which are believed to be the spoken essence of the universe in Buddhism and Hinduism, to further relax your mind and to set the intention of having a deep meditation.

If you find yourself having difficulty going beyond your thoughts, try to visualize a calm place. It can be a white sandy beach, or a door that opens to a beautiful, empty sky. Visualize it until your body and mind are relaxed and at rest. Allow the silence to unfold.

Notice that the silence is very much alive, and resonant. Allow your awareness to remain on the silence. You may start to feel expansive, as if you are somehow moving beyond your ordinary confines, and coming into union with the silence. Now you are one with the silence. Now you are free from your conditioned path.

This is a glimpse of your authentic self. It is the beginning of an endlessly deep and satisfying experience of who you truly are. It is a place of transformation, from being in a state of distracted thought to being in a state of both inner and outer harmony.

In the Messenger

"A New Earth: Awakening to Your Life's Purpose" by Eckhart Tolle, "Zen Mind, Beginner's Mind" by Shunryu Suzuki, and "Emptiness Dancing" by Adyashanti: these are all very popular books that show how unique each person's experience of enlightenment and authentic self-expression can be. They all point to the same wisdom and knowing from different perspectives. The difficulty we have as an audience is in being able to remain focused and clear, to have a stable experience, while trying to follow these various examples of how to bring the authentic self to light.

Every person has a unique way of thinking, feeling, and acting in the world, an intimate way of experiencing and expressing the truth, but there are gaps that exist between what we know to be true and how well we are able to communicate this knowing. Members of the same family, couples who have lived together for years, friends and neighbors and co-workers all share the challenging task of trying to bridge this gap, often resulting in some form of confusion.

Think of the game known as telephone. In this game, as many players as possible line up to whisper a message from the beginning of the line to the end of the line. Usually, the message that the last player calls out is completely different from the original message and we all have a good laugh. It is important to realize that we rarely understand the message intended by the speaker who is communicating it. Even if we do hear the correct words spoken, we will still interpret them through our own personal and unique contexts and images.

We may not know what the Buddha actually meant when he said, "Fill your mind with compassion." We may not know what Jesus meant when he said, "It is easier for a camel to pass through the eye of a needle, than for a rich man to enter the kingdom of heaven." While these sayings may hold value for some of us, they do not necessarily bring us any closer to God, the authentic self, or enlightenment. They are simply the expressions of those who have already realized that their own authentic voice is extraordinary and unique.

When you discover your own authentic voice, you may also have your own sayings to share with the world. You too will discover your own way of expressing your authentic self, because you will see that you too are the essence of God's work. Your own experiences and expressions are neither more of nor less than that of anyone who has come before you. You are authentically you. Look at it, and see it. Know it. Know your own mind. Know your own feelings. Know your own actions. Know your own authentic self. This is self-realization, which is what enlightenment is all about. The teaching is that enlightenment comes from within one's own experience. It is always beautiful and unique. The teaching is not in the message – it is in the messenger, and the messenger is you.

The Center of Existence

Imagine what life might look like without you in it. Imagine taking yourself out of your own life. Notice that the ability to do so is only within your own imagination. In truth, you simply cannot remove yourself – you exist, and are always at the center of your own existence.

Every sensation that you perceive, every thought or feeling, happens within your field of awareness. You are the one who is aware of this field of sensations. Life as we know it is not possible without you being in it, exactly as you are. Every sensation in life arises within and falls away from your field of awareness. A thought comes and goes. A feeling comes and goes. A moment in time comes and goes. You have created all of these sensations to have an experience of existence. They appear to and fall away from you.

This is difficult for our minds to comprehend, because our minds work in the realm of thought and imagination, and we are talking about the truth. The truth is not a thought or something that is imagined. It can only be known through the direct experience of each and every moment.

Take a moment to consciously experience it for yourself. Look around you. Notice that you are the one who is aware of everything that is perceived. Every sight and sound, thought and feeling arises within your field of awareness. What you are aware of may change, but your field of awareness, that which contains these changes, does not. You can play with this by opening and closing your eyes, or cupping and uncupping your ears with your hands. Notice that although these changes are taking place, you, as an observer of these changes within your field of awareness, remain the same, untouched.

What you do in life matters the most to you – it is your experience, your truth. You are creating it. Every experience that you perceive is appearing to you. You have the power to consciously affect change over all of it. Seeing through the game of life is simply the knowing in each moment that you are the center of your own existence. Whether you choose to create an enjoyable life or one of hardship has only to do with your understanding of how much power you actually have over the creation of your own experience.

∞ ② ∞

Practice Idea: Posture Towards Life

Your life is a reflection of you. Life responds instantly to your attitude towards it, and your physical posture is a good indication of the various thoughts and feelings that you may be having. Your posture towards life is one of the best indications of how life is responding to you.

Try looking at yourself in a mirror. Notice your posture. Notice the expression on your face. Your thoughts and feelings will be different if you simply change your posture. If your arms are crossed, try holding them out in front of you. If your expression is tired or sad, try smiling, without judging yourself for it.

Try to smile even if you do not feel like smiling. You are safe. No one is here to judge you for smiling at yourself, and if you continue to smile, you will soon feel happiness sneaking into your thoughts and emotions. You may even start to laugh.

Notice that your attitude is changing. Your posture towards life is shifting in a positive way. Sometimes, to have a *break-through*, we simply need to *break-out* of a posture towards life that is not serving us. If you move in life with this new posture or attitude, you will find that you attract new friendships and opportunities. What was once unavailable to you, may now open up and become accessible, because you have shifted your posture towards life.

The Right Word

We are in a constant state of communication with each other and within our own minds, using the signs and symbols of our respective cultures and time period. We use analogies, metaphors, and symbolism in our most basic forms of communication.

We generally take for granted our fluent understanding of the relationship among these signs and the things they refer to, as well as the effects that they have on us. Mark Twain said that "the difference between the almost right word and the right word is really a large matter – it's the difference between the lightning bug and the lightning."

This illustrates the power of language. Along the path to discovering the authentic self, common words and phrases that we come across include *compassion*, *love*, *presence*, *resonance*, *higher self*, *in-the-now*, *lovingkindness*, *fear*, *desire*, and *ego*. These references are the signs and symbols used in most spiritual teachings, and we naturally try to connect them to their implied meanings, but in the context of enlightenment they are always, as Mark Twain says, "the almost right word," which is "really a large matter."

Spiritual teachers admit to this disconnection all of the time. There is a vast difference between the words being used and the experiences they attempt to describe. We hear the words, think that we have an understanding of what they mean, and attempt to attain a way of being that reflects our understanding of them. Our first mistake is in trying to attain a way of being that is only understood by the person who is attempting to describe it. Our second mistake is in thinking that we need to attain some other way of being to have self-realization, to be enlightened.

We may ask ourselves, "What would the Buddha do?" We may say to ourselves, "I should have more compassion for this person, or that situation." But if these thoughts do not arise from our own authentic experience in the present moment, then they will be weak and misguided, because they will only represent a conditioned misunderstanding of what another person has referred to as an aspect of enlightenment.

Your authentic self can only communicate about compassion, love, presence, and connection through your own experiences of these, in your words, your own vision of truth. It is important that we do not get too caught up in the words and phrases that others have used to describe enlightenment. Simply knowing that your authentic self communicates in its own unique way is one of the pillars of self-realization.

The Truth to Unfold

Most people would not recognize Jesus if they saw him walking down the street. To recognize what is divine within someone else, we need to be able to see what is divine within ourselves. When we know our own divinity, we are able to see it reflected back to us from within everyone and everything. This is the embodiment of perfection that Jesus represents, and what Buddhists refer to as the perfection of wisdom.

All paths lead to one road, and each of us have our own way of allowing the truth to unfold, regardless of our apparent differences. What each of us come to see in our own way is that we are not who we think we are, and who we think we are will never be satisfied by what it is looking for and finds. We are not here to perform any miracles, but to observe the miracles that already exist before our very own eyes.

Our capacity to experience different forms of existence, including the experience of nonexistence, is endless, because we can have any and all experiences that we are open to having. If a person believes that they are everything, they can look for themselves through the experience of being everything, and at some point find that this is true. If a person believes that they are nothing, they can perform the same search until they discover how this is also true.

All of which begs a simple, yet powerful question: *who* cares? Why make such an effort, when we do not even know who it serves? These questions may arise if we become aware of the fact that we are trying to find something that is already within our own possession, the authentic self.

Years ago, I went with my family to see a meteor shower. It was a beautiful dark night, the sky was crystal clear, and every few seconds a meteor would light up the horizon. I remember that almost every time a meteor appeared, someone would say "Wow, look over there," and one of us would look just a little too late to see anything. Then the next meteor would light up the sky, and someone else would have the experience of just missing it. Someone would point, all of us would look, and it seemed to me like one of us would just never quite get to see it.

This experience is similar to what the mind does. It looks and points in all directions for reality, but seems to just miss it, which keeps us in the action of looking, rather than in the aspect of seeing. Our minds play out this game – one that is designed to keep us preoccupied, locked up in a system of thought, spinning around in circles – such that while we are busy looking, we do not see what is right in front of us. We miss seeing truth, awareness, wisdom, and love . . . and that we are entirely whole and perfect in every way.

In this true seeing, many internal and external conflicts are resolved. The relief of this experience is what allows us to fully embrace the external world. It is a type of relaxed embrace that is powerful, yet gentle and sweet. Simply notice that you are aware of everything that arises within and falls away from your field of awareness. From this point of observation, see that you have access to your own wisdom at all times. See that you are love embodied, inseparable from all of creation and therefore entirely connected to every aspect of it – a divining rod of truth. Relax deeply into this seeing, to fully enjoy and appreciate your life.

∞ ②⟩ ∞

Practice Idea: Create a Mandala

A mandala is a symbolic representation of the nature of existence. It is often used as a form of meditation. Its symbolic nature is seen as a way of accessing deeper levels of the unconscious self, allowing its creator to experience the mystery of life.

This exercise can be performed by anyone of any age. You do not need to have a single artistic bone in your body to create this type of mandala – just a pen and paper, and some crayons to add color.

Hold the edge of the paper with one hand, and have the pen ready with the other hand. Close your eyes. For approximately one minute of time, draw one continuous, topsy-turvy line without lifting the pen. Now open your eyes.

Randomly choose a crayon, and starting with the smallest segments, begin to color in each one. Try to avoid using the same color on two adjacent segments. You can choose another random color to use at any time. The purpose of selecting colors at random is to allow your subconscious mind to be an active participant in creating your mandala.

You may notice some interesting thoughts or feelings that arise as you are coloring in your mandala. You may even find that some answers to questions which previously eluded you are now clear, or that the whole dilemma has simply gone away.

Look at the mandala once it has been completely colored in. Observe it from different angles. Everything that you see is a representation of yourself. It is an expression of your unconscious self communicating with your conscious self, to create an experience of your whole self. It is an important connection to make if we wish to discover more about the mystery of life and our existence.

"Dream lofty dreams, and as you dream,
so shall you become. Your Vision is the promise
of what you shall one day be.
Your Ideal is the prophecy of what
you shall at last unveil."

~James Allen

3

A Self-Fulfilling Prophecy

A self-fulfilling prophecy is the belief in a prediction that causes itself to become true due to the simple fact that the prediction was made. Our beliefs influence our actions, and cause the prediction to fulfill itself. Enlightenment is a self-fulfilling prophecy that begins with an awakening. We awaken to the journey of enlightenment.

An awakening is a moment in which some aspect of our authentic self that was once hidden is now revealed. It is the A-ha! moment of spontaneous self-realization. An awakening is a prediction of our own enlightenment, and will naturally fulfill itself as we begin to believe and act as though it will come true, although it will do so in ways we least expect.

Seeing through the game of life is an awakening experience that can arise slowly to deliver a powerful insight, or it can suddenly deliver an eye-opening truth . . . either way, what we realize about our authentic self was previously unknown to us, and the way we move in life afterwards will be slightly or significantly changed.

Through an awakening experience, we may realize that we are nothing. We may realize that we are everything. We may realize that we are timeless and eternal. We may realize some of the essential human aspects of our being, such as wisdom, love, and peace. The possibilities are truly endless and deep. The awakening experience will eventually come to pass – as all experiences are God's way of breathing in and out, arising within our field of awareness and then falling away – but what always remains is a profound impression of what has just been experienced and realized.

We will most likely try to understand the experience more fully, in the context of our lives. What does this mean? How does this happen? Will this happen again? All of these questions are an indication that we are now on a journey toward the self-fulfilling prophecy of enlightenment. As we search for answers to these questions, we walk along a new path that is now available to us, one that will continue to bring an endless stream of awakening experiences that come and go.

Your Own Heart and Eyes

Inside each and every one of us is the knowing that life is our own creation, regardless of whether it appears to be calm and flowing, rigid or difficult. Whether we are open and content, or shut down and turned away . . . life is our creation. It is not the creation of the ego, who we believe ourselves to be, but that of our authentic self. Our authentic self creates a multitude of experiences for us to have and learn from, and when we are aware of this, we are able to actualize a tremendous power of influence over our own lives.

I remember a time when I was at war within myself. There was so much conflict within my own mind. My ego, my persona, continuously spoke to me about the past and all the knowledge we had gained, in anticipation of what it promised the future would hold for me. I was often fooled into listening to and believing in these stories, as they would compete for my energy and attention, which I gave fully to the most convincing. Again and again, I was disappointed and conflicted, in an argument with God and myself.

Then something stirred from the depths of my being, independent of these thoughts and stories; Something that knew better than to believe in them: my authentic self. I sensed that we were one and the same. I knew instantly that I had been fooled by my own ego a million times or more. I felt awake to this knowing. Awake to the thoughts. Awake to the conflict.

I used the power of my authentic self to see through all of the false ideas and beliefs that my ego had constructed and was invested in . . . and at long last, I felt at peace, at rest. The warmth of a deep love grew within my chest. I looked out, into life, and could see through it, as though it were an illusion, a beautiful illusion. I saw a tree, a street filled with cars, someone talking on a cell phone, a bicyclist passing by. My wife was playing with our children, and they held hands to cross the street. As I turned away from the sun, I felt a touch of coldness upon my arms, and in that moment, I knew myself to be a divine being, having a human experience in a world of illusions.

Your authentic self also knows that life is an illusion that appears to and falls away from you. It knows that you are the only one who is capable of creating and destroying your thoughts and stories. You are the one that believes in them or does not. You have most likely lived a thousand different lives, in just as many forms. You are connected to all beings as well as connected to God. This knowing is asserted in the experience of awakening to your authentic self. It is what keeps the warring ego, or persona, at bay and in check.

We all have various experiences that validate the same knowing. Our hearts and eyes may feel and see differently, but what they know is the same. Life is beautiful and fleeting. Soften your gaze and share in the experience. Watch as it unfolds. Embrace it. Steep yourself in the mystery of it. Look it directly in the eyes. You just might even end up laughing.

∞ 🦢 ∞

Practice Idea: Intentional Prayer

"May all human beings have the grace to accept with serenity the things that cannot be changed, courage to change the things which should be changed, and the wisdom to know the difference.

May we live one day at a time, and enjoy each moment as it comes: accepting hardships as a pathway to peace, taking this world as it is, not as we would have it, trusting that all things are right, and that we may be happy in this life, and in those to come. So be it."

~Anicius Boethius

Intentional prayer can be a powerful tool. It holds the capacity to transform our lives in ways that we could never imagine, through the strength of our own conviction to bring it to life. To paraphrase Ghandi, "Be the prayer that you want to see in the world."

Intentional prayer is an indication of our being open to change. It acknowledges that many aspects of life are out of our control. Through intentional prayer, we seek knowledge and understanding which has been previously unknown to us, so that we can change in the ways that support our prayers. We can open our own hearts and eyes through the power of intentional prayer.

Nothing is Personal

Seeing through the game of life is the knowing that nothing is personal. When we do not take our experiences personally, we can see them for what they are – energy. The world is a movement of energy. You are a human being, comprised of energy. You breathe life into your body and sustain it through energy. Your emotions are various forms of energy that come and go, in the same way that thoughts do. There is nothing personal about any of this, and we are all participating in every aspect of it.

When we personalize an experience, we are placing an emphasis on containing it within the perspective of our own minds, and focusing on a way of looking at it that is partial and limited. A personal way of seeing and understanding life is not in alignment with the truth.

We can give ourselves a sense of being isolated from the natural world if we begin to think and feel that we are somehow separate from life. We may believe that what happens in nature is not personal, but what happens to us is. Our reasoning alludes to this sense of separation from the natural world.

We know that when an earthquake destroys a city, it does not do so with personal intent. It just happens, naturally. We acknowledge that a greater force is at work. But when one human being hurts another, we view this as a personal attack. On one hand, an attacker is personally responsible and will be held accountable for his or her actions – human beings have a capacity to make choices regarding the use of their energy in ways that the earth does not; on the other hand, the same non-personal source of energy that funds the movement of the earth and that of thought is truly responsible for all matters that occur: namely, God.

Our limited perspective does not immediately recognize that just as the planet contains a natural force of energy that can lead to an earthquake, so do our bodies and minds contain a natural force of energy that can lead to conflict. Both arise from the same intelligence and source. This does not mean that the energy of conflict should be condoned, only that we do not need to suffer even more by personalizing the experience of it.

The energy of our thoughts and feelings as they come flooding through in times of conflict can be likened to that of an earthquake. Both are naturally occurring. Neither one is personal; although we, as human beings, have the capacity to cultivate the intelligent use of this energy when it arises – it can happen to any one of us.

Being In Equanimity

The word equanimity is defined as being levelheaded, calm, and happy. It is a state of inner peace. The outer world is simply a reflection of the inner world . . . thus it will also be experienced as a state of outer peace. If you are in a state of inner peace, the outer world, no matter how busy it may seem, will feel tranquil.

Look for a peaceful external environment to assist you in finding the same quite place within. Take a moment to slow down and become mindful of what you are physically doing. We can enter into a state of equanimity through conscious observation.

∞ 2) ∞

Practice Idea: Conscious Observation

Conscious observation is a form of the Buddhist practice known as mindfulness. In this exercise, we will focus our awareness on what we are physically doing in the present moment, instead of listening to any mind chatter that comes up.

Since mind chatter is typically an emotional response to past events, engaging it tends to shift our awareness away from what we are doing in the present moment. We want to simply pay no attention to the mind chatter and focus all of our awareness on what we are physically doing. You will feel a heightened sense of being awake during this practice, because your awareness will be unified in its focus on the present moment.

Start by finding a quiet place in a natural setting, such as a little grove or a patch of grass. Hold your hands out in front of you. Allow yourself to become fully absorbed by the experience of being with your hands. Look at them and feel them.

Now close your eyes. Observe the silence. Open your eyes. Observe your hands. Know the experience deeply for what it is. Close your eyes, emptiness. Open your eyes, existence.

Notice the light that surrounds your hands, as they appear to be more vivid and bright. Now move your observation away from your hands and toward the natural elements of your environment.

Notice the profound light and colors that emanate from a nearby tree or blade of grass. What was once ordinary, may now seem extraordinary. This is being in the present moment. You have now entered into a state of equanimity.

Try to use this mindfulness practice to access this state of equanimity throughout the day. You can become aware of your hands while sitting in traffic. You can become aware of your feet while going for a jog. There are so many opportunities to practice this technique, so use it as often as you can.

A Vast Difference

There is often a vast difference between what we do and who we truly are. It is the difference between doing love and being love. The first is conditioned and the second is inherent. One is learned, while the other is an essential aspect of our true nature. This difference exists unless, of course, what we do is in alignment with our authentic self – but this is rarely the case, as most of us have forgotten who we truly are.

If we take off the mask, and let the disguise called *me* fall to the ground, we are simply left with awareness: the awareness of an exterior world of images and actions, and of an interior world of thoughts and feelings in motion. We may also be aware of the vibrant resonance often referred to as life force. Essentially, we are aware of the physical, mental, and spiritual aspects of being human.

In honor of this awareness, a sense of love emerges from deep within your heart. It is not a feeling of love, but a knowing of love. It does not come from an act of loving, but from the experience of being love itself. It is not bound by any circumstance or condition that may arise in life. It is simply love. This is an aspect of your true nature. It is an inherent quality of abiding in your authentic self. This experience, like all other experiences, will likely come and go. When it goes, the natural tendency to *do* love may occur, as we are no longer in a place of *being* love. This is what happens when we try to hold on to an experience that has already passed.

Doing love will usually take on the misguided shape of trying to love everyone and everything. It is an extremely common occurrence that happens in many spiritual circles. Being love will take any form that it chooses, because it is totally free from attachment to anything in life: it exists before, during, and after life. This is true love. It does not change. It is an essential aspect of our true nature. Just as the sun can be felt in the absence of a breeze, so too can we experience true love in the absence of conditional loving.

An Effortless Embrace

Enlightenment is not a state of being. A state of being is something that can and will be subject to change. Our thoughts are a state of being. Our emotions are a state of being. Enlightenment is an exploration of the fundamental tenets of being human that do not change, such as the authentic self, our true nature, and pure awareness.

Awareness does not change. What you are aware of changes, but awareness itself remains the same. Your authentic self always remains, timeless and eternal. Your true nature is without fear or judgment, and embraces the awareness of all internal and external experiences at once, as they occur in the present moment.

It is simply not possible to use your thoughts to embrace anything. A thought does not embrace – it reflects. It can reflect the act of embracing something, such as acknowledging *I embrace your opinion*, but even this statement reflects the fact that *I* am actually doing the embracing, not the thought itself.

Most of us rely heavily upon our thoughts as an essential way of experiencing the world. We often mistake what it is that has the capacity to embrace. We do not need to actively embrace anything, because our true nature is already doing so, through awareness. If you carefully observe this truth you will see that there is nothing more to do. There is no part of you that could possibly stop yourself from being aware all of the time. It is awareness that has the innate capacity to embrace everything.

When you are conscious of this natural ability to embrace every experience through awareness, your mind will stop trying to do the work for you. Your mind will come to rest in the absence of trying to present you with a problem to solve. Your mind will see that the work has already been finished. Actually, it will see that the work was never really necessary. Now you can relax and deeply settle into yourself. This is one of many entry points into the heart of self-realization.

Resting in our natural way of being is very blissful. It is an experience of our true nature that comes from not having resistance to life, and being able to relax deeply into each moment. Bliss is being in communication with life without the weight of resistance. Have you ever had a wonderful conversation with another person, one that seemed to flow back and forth effortlessly? That effortless flow is a gateway to the experience of bliss. It mirrors our true nature of being in harmony with life, and accepting the world we live in.

There is a moment in the process of dying that is equally blissful. It occurs when we are hanging over the edge of death, clinging to that last rock of life, and losing strength with every effort to hold on. We are soon forced to let go, and enter into the flow of dying, as we no longer have the strength to resist it. This moment is extremely blissful. There is also a kind of death that we can undergo in life, by fully letting go.

Having Resistance

Standing in a moment of truth is like releasing a giant floodgate. We are wide open, exposed. Anything that has been held back and everything that wants to be released will come rushing through this gate with a force to be reckoned with. The moment can feel extremely overwhelming if it is one of our first experiences of standing in truth.

You may not be prepared to face the fear of death, the ignorance of judgment, or the pain of separation in one fell swoop. You may try to close the floodgate. Just remember that this moment only comes to those who are truly ready to have it. Even so, your natural inclination may be to resist this onset of truth and the motion toward a complete release.

Over ten years ago, after having a series of profound awakening experiences, I went to see my spiritual teacher at his home. We were already friends at the time and he was familiar with the experiences that troubled me.

My teacher was at the side of his house trying to open the bathroom window, because he was locked out. I volunteered to squeeze through the open window, and unlocked the front door. We stood in the garden in front of his house, where I told him that I was having resistance – major resistance. He responded by asking me to look around, and to see that everything was having resistance. I looked around the garden and seemed to know exactly what he meant.

There was a natural resistance all around us. The flowers in the garden resisted gravity and the earth. Tiny drops of dew resisted the petals they were perched upon. Moving cars on the street resisted stillness. The noise that they made resisted silence. My own life resisted death. The movement of these thoughts occurred to me in resistance to the stillness of my being. Every thought that was seen in the foreground of my mind, seemed to resist an opposing thought in the background: *me* and *you*, subject and object, resistance and acceptance.

My awareness then shifted, to knowing myself as one subject observing many objects of thought. Everything was contained within a unified field of awareness. I looked at both resistance and acceptance and saw them as a parent sees two opposing children. Both were seen and embraced equally, simultaneously. Both dropped away in that very moment.

When we are able to shift our focus, step back and know that all experiences exist within the greater context of awareness, we can see that there is nothing to do but simply allow them to be as they are. In the absence of opposition, thoughts fall away quite naturally.

What I learned from my spiritual teacher is that not having resistance to being in resistance is the fastest way to let go, to stand in a moment of truth; and that shimmying though a bathroom window to unlock your front door, may be the fastest way to getting back into your house once you have been locked out.

The Desire to Change

The desire to change stems from a feeling of being incomplete no matter what we do. It comes from a deep sense of missing something in life. Whether we know it or not, there is a general dissatisfaction with every short-lived pleasure that we experience, and we are looking for something that will give us a lasting sense of fulfillment.

We are mostly unconscious to this sense of fundamentally missing something important, and often experience it is as a kinesthetic feeling of anxiety or stress, heartache, headache, or even a belly ache. All we know is that we feel something is not quite right, and we tend to look outside of ourselves for some form of resolution. We may think that another friendship, car, outfit, or even another pet will solve the problem, because these may have in the past, momentarily. The more we search outside of ourselves for a solution, the more we feel incomplete and discontent, which drives us further into a sense of separation.

This sense of separation can be powerful enough to fill us with a desire to become more conscious of its origin and cause. Through a process of questioning the experience by trial and error, we begin to more fully understand it: it is not caused by this, not caused by that . . . not this, not that.

At this point, we have an opportunity to realize that both the desire to change and the sense of fundamentally missing something important come from not knowing the truth of our existence: our authentic self. This realization can allow us to feel contentment, a sense of being complete, and can create a lasting sense of relief if it is experienced deeply. We may have failed to see this truth a thousand times, but it only takes one tangible success to make a lasting impression.

∞ ⟨2⟩ ∞

Practice Idea: Daily Rituals

A ritual is a ceremony, practice, or act that is designed to remind us to cultivate a particular skill or awareness. It is chosen for its ability to bring about the actual experience that we are trying to learn from. If you apply yourself fully to a well-designed ritual, you will see immediate results via its performance, and those results will happen as often as you decide to perform the ritual.

To understand something, it is helpful to first practice it. Through the practice of a ritual, you will become aware of why it is set up the way that it is. The strength of a ritual will come forth when you engage in it fully, with your whole body and mind.

For the purpose of knowing the truth of your existence, your authentic self, you may need to be fully aware of a ritual that is designed to give you that experience. There are many traditions with numerous rituals that are created to help you know your authentic self.

Some rituals instruct us to chant a certain verse, or light a candle with a certain intention. Regardless of the explanations we use for practicing a ritual, we want it to ultimately serve the purpose of helping us realize the truth of our existence and our authentic self.

An extremely powerful ritual that can be incorporated into your daily routine is the chanting of the Buddhist Heart Sutra. The Heart Sutra is often used in the opening and closing of Buddhist ceremonies, and can be easily recited at the beginning and ending of a meditation, in order to set the intention of self-realization. If you do this on a regular basis, you will see many positive changes in your life that will appear to happen on their own.

The Heart Sutra:

"Form is no different from emptiness. Emptiness is no different from form. That which is form is emptiness. That which is emptiness is form.

Feelings, perceptions, impulses, consciousness, the same is true of these. All truths are marked with emptiness. They do not appear or disappear, are not tainted or pure, do not increase or decrease. Therefore in emptiness there is:

No form, feelings, perceptions, impulses, or consciousness. No eyes, ears, nose, tongue, body, or mind. No color, sound, smell, taste, touch, or object of mind.

No realm of eyes, and so forth, until there is no realm of mind consciousness. No ignorance and also no extinction of ignorance, and so forth, until no old age and death, and no extinction of old age and death. No suffering, origination, stopping, or path. No cognition and no attainment.

With nothing to attain, the enlightened being depends upon The Perfection of Wisdom. The mind is no hindrance. Without any hindrance no fear can exist. Far apart from every inverted view (s)he dwells in Nirvana.

All enlightened beings past, present and future rely on The Perfection of Wisdom and live in full enlightenment.

The Perfection of Wisdom is the great transcendent mantra. It is the supreme mantra that removes all suffering. This is the truth. Say it so: Gone. Gone. Gone beyond. Gone fully beyond. Awakened! So be it!"

~Gautam Buddha

Know Thyself

There is an ancient Greek saying inscribed at the Temple of Apollo in Delphi, Greece: *Know Thyself.* It is a principal teaching and guiding rule that has been used by many influential figures, including Plato, Socrates, Alexander Pope, Benjamin Franklin, and Ralph Waldo Emerson.

To *know thyself* is to know that life is spiritual. It is to know that human beings are spiritual. It is to know that your life and humanity are both expressions of God's spirit in form and function. Know yourself to be the living expression of this fundamental truth, to enable yourself to live a full and satisfying life in each and every moment, regardless of whether you show up as a doctor in New York, a school teacher in Minnesota, a chef in Maui, or a cab driver in Los Angeles.

To identify the difference between a sweet pepper and a spicy pepper is intelligent, but to identify the difference between a so-called *ordinary* experience and a *spiritual* experience is unfortunate. It shows that we know more about peppers than we do about ourselves. When we identify with one experience as being *ordinary*, with a host of qualities that we believe to represent that experience, and another as *spiritual*, with its own set of qualities, we are essentially dividing a wholesome experience of being human into fractions and parts.

It is like being identified with the belief that your own two hands are somehow not connected to your body. It is to be filled with a constant sense of desire that can never be fully satisfied, and the need to move on from one experience to the next. When you *know thyself*, you possess a complete awareness of God moving through you, a lasting sense of fulfillment. The spirit of God may be moved by what you think or how you act, but it is only truly and deeply touched by who you know yourself to be . . . so *know thyself* in each and every moment.

"You are the deepest wisdom and the Highest truth;
the greatest peace and the grandest love. You are
these things. And in moments of your life you have
known yourself to be these things. Choose now to know
yourself as these things always."

~Neale Donald Walsch

4

The Ultimate Truth

Those of us who choose to "know ourselves as these things always" have come by many paths to the same place. The names we give to this place and the symbols we use for it may be different, but it is the same place nonetheless. We conceive of it differently because what is happening cannot truly be described, and what is being described does not truly reflect what is happening. You may say that it is like a gate that opens to heaven, when there is no gate at all. Someone else might think of it differently, such as a flower that is always opening to life and itself. The symbols that we choose are our own closest representation of something that cannot be fully known or described. Seeing through the game of life is the knowing that these signs and symbols are our best possible way of understanding and communicating our experiences.

A Vision of God

"Since we are dealing with invisible and unknowable things (for God is beyond human understanding, and there is no means of proving immortality) . . . There is a strong empirical reason why we should cultivate thoughts that can never be proved, it is that they are known to be useful."

~Carl Jung

God is the symbol of a divine experience that lies beyond our ability to completely understand or communicate. When we have a vision of God or heaven, we are connecting to our own unique way of being with a transcendent experience. My own experience of this once happened with a vision of God's feet.

As my eyes were closed in meditation, a sensation of bliss overcame my body, and the image of a shining flight of stairs appeared before me. My awareness quickly ascended the heavenly stairway to its very peak, where I was met by the vision of an intense brilliant light that I knew to be God.

I was kept from looking directly at God by the intensity of light and bliss that I experienced; however, my gaze was able to remain upon what appeared to me as God's feet. For how long I stayed in this state of being was beyond me. At some point, my awareness descended the shining flight of stairs and maintained a deep meditative state of bliss.

At the time, I had no experience with these types of visions, and therefore no way of understanding it. I truly was not sure if it was somehow real or just imagined. After years of exploring these types of visions, I have come know them as my own symbolic representation of what I can never fully understand (God). Such is the nature of these visions, as they are unique to each of us. We all have a symbolic vision and expression of our own divinity that represents an ability to transcend what is ordinary and known.

∞ 2 ∞

Practice Idea: Active Imagination

Active imagination is a concept developed by the famous psychologist Carl Jung. It is a method of exploring the unknown through the signs and symbols of dreams, imagination, and fantasy. It can bridge the gap between the conscious and unconscious aspects of the mind, helping to promote the development of self-realization.

Active imagination techniques include forms of dance, music, painting, and drama. Various types of oracle prophecy that allow us to gain knowledge which is not available through ordinary means are also included, such as divination with cards or the reading of tea leaves.

The following multi-step active imagination technique has the capacity to resolve many of the paradoxes that exist in the mind.

* First, meditate. It is more effective to engage your inner self from a state of silence. In meditation, you can decrease or even suspend the chatter of your mind.

* Next, invite. Invite an image to appear or use an image from your imagination or from one of your dreams or fantasies. Any image that comes from the unconscious mind will carry a sense that you did not create it. You may even question where it came from. Invite the image to speak to you or to move on its own, without trying to control it.

* Next, dialogue. Have a conversation with the image. Be sure to keep your attention on the image while being in conversation with it. If your attention moves away from the original image, you are no longer in active imagination.

* Finally, analyze. Record any and all information that is received through your dialogue. Often the information that you receive can be difficult to express through ordinary means, so you may need to express it through movement, painting, poetry, or even storytelling. Now judge the value of the information by analyzing it in the context of common sense. Remember that you are basically trying to integrate your head with your heart.

Everything and Nothing

All sensations arise within our field of awareness. When we observe this truth, a profound question may arise: *who is watching this happen?* There is no way to easily answer this question through words and concepts – every answer, including the question itself, arises within our field of awareness. The only way to answer the question is to have a direct experience of presence for oneself.

Take a moment to look around yourself What do you see? Notice that what you see changes as you move your gaze. What do you hear? Notice that what you hear also changes. How do you feel? Notice that what you feel is changing.

Simply notice all of these sensations and all of these changes. Now you are in the present moment.

You are now observing each experience as it arises from moment to moment. Notice that everything you observe happens within this field of awareness. There is no denying this or escaping from it when you are present. Now ask the question: *Who am I?* Notice that the answer is in the actual experience.

You are everything and nothing. You are everything that you observe within your field of awareness, and the mysterious nothingness of God that seems to be watching it all happen. You are both subject and object. There is no division. There is no separation. Both are happening, simultaneously.

Think of it like the story of the Buddha and his disciple Mahakasyapa. Near the end of his life, the Buddha would quietly gather with his disciples before a lotus pond. The disciples would sit in a circle to receive the Buddha's teachings. One day, the Buddha sat silently with his followers: no words came to him. He pulled a lotus from the pond. This beautiful flower dripped with muck and water.

The Buddha presented it to each follower, who in turn did their best to explain what the dripping lotus flower symbolized and how it fit into the Buddha's teachings. Then the Buddha came to his disciple Mahakasyapa. Mahakasyapa instantly understood it to mean that the dripping murk of life and the flowering of enlightenment are intertwined. He smiled and then laughed.

The Buddha handed the lotus flower to Mahakasyapa and began to speak to his followers. He said, "What can be said I have said to you. And what cannot be said I have given to Mahakashyapa." What "can be said" is the experience of everything. What "cannot be said" is the experience of nothing. This is what is meant by saying that we are both everything and nothing.

The Continuum

Life is a continuum, an expansive myriad of the infinite forms of existence that go on and on, indefinitely. It is a single door that opens to ten other doors, each opening to ten more, so on and so forth, endlessly so. Birth is what happens when we step through one door and death is what happens when we step through the next. Our existence is always continuous. This truth is easily reflected back to us by nature.

The revered Buddhist monk Thich Nhat Hanh reminds us that "nothing comes from nothing. Before its so-called birth, the flower already existed in other forms – clouds, sunshine, seeds, soil, and many other elements. Rather than birth and rebirth, it is more accurate to say 'manifestation' and 'remanifestation'. The so-called birthday of the flower is really a day of its remanifestation. It has already been here in other forms, and now it has made an effort to remanifest."

The word *Maya* (meaning "illusion" in Sanskrit) is used to describe the appearance of all forms of life. It is also used to describe things that are not really as they seem. Life is *Maya*. Our perception of life is also *Maya*.

Human beings perceive the world through the five senses: touch, smell, taste, vision, and hearing. If we lose one of our senses, such as vision or hearing, we will perceive life differently. What seems real to us will be different with vision than it is without vision.

When the Spanish conquistadors arrived in North America, many Native Americans described an inability to see the foreign ships. There are accounts made by Native Americans of only being able to hear the strange sound of the ocean waves breaking in an unfamiliar pattern. When the Native Americans did see the conquistadors and their ships, they conceived of them as gods arriving on heavenly structures. In the same respect, a person who does not sense the presence of spirits will most likely decide that they are not real, whereas a person who does sense the presence of these entities will decide that they are real. Just because we do not perceive something with our senses does not mean that it is not present or real. These are examples of *Maya*, the illusion of life that is created by our own unique senses and perception of existence.

Consider the story of an ancient Indian guru who was placed in captivity and faced a death sentence, for teaching others about the nature of *Maya* and the misperceptions of the time. As the old man quietly sat before his impending execution, one of his captors felt moved by compassion to stay and tend to his needs.

In the evening of the first night, the captor looked into the cell and saw that the old man was not there. The guru had miraculously disappeared. In the morning, he reappeared.

In the evening of the second night, the captor could not seem to perceive the cell in which the old man sat. The whole cell had miraculously disappeared. In the morning, it reappeared, with the guru in it.

In the evening of the third night, the captor could not seem to perceive himself. All awareness of his known self had disappeared. In the morning, he too reappeared.

That morning, the captor said to the old guru, "Master, now I see the truth of your teachings. There is no reality other than God. Tell me, why do you stay here to die?" The guru responded, "What is born, must also die – but we do not. This is the natural way."

We Live On

We are immortal beings – drops of water falling from the sky, the rush of wind blowing through a pasture of grass, a bird taking flight. Regardless of the forms we take on, there is no beginning and no end to our own existence, and we have, through a multitude of transformations, cultivated the ability to manifest as human beings. Most of us have lived many lifetimes as a human being. Our souls are profoundly touched by the experiences of each lifetime, and have access to all past life information and experience.

You are an aspect of God, and as such, have access to all of God's wisdom and grace. Your quality of life can be tremendously full and complete when you are in touch with this knowing. Awakenings, mystical experiences, and enlightenment are all twists and turns that we take along the path to discovering the authentic self – your immortal self, that which is connected to everything and everyone, and has access to all information at all times.

∞ ❧ ∞

Practice Idea: Past Life Meditation

Discovering a past life can be an amazing experience. It can hold new insights that directly relate to the life lessons that you are currently working on. This past life meditation will allow you to explore all of your past lives, in as much depth as you choose, and return to them as often as you would like.

First relax your body in a quiet place. Take a few deep breaths. Notice the energy in your body as it gently moves from head to toe. Feel the lightness of being in your body, as you relax.

With your eyes closed, imagine a room. It seems to surround you with a warm golden light that makes you feel safe and protected. Now look at the walls and notice that there are pictures everywhere. Each picture is of a person. Your own picture is directly in front of you. You realize that the other pictures are of your past selves, taken in different lives, at different times and places.

Have a look at as many pictures as you would like to see. Notice that some pictures draw your attention more than others. These pictures seem to emit a certain quality of white light. Allow your awareness to be drawn to one of these pictures, and notice that it seems to come alive before your very eyes. You seem to be able to taste, touch, and feel the very essence of the picture as it comes to life.

Now take a moment to look at the past life that has drawn your attention. Experience and explore it as fully as you would like to. Know that you can leave and return to it at any time, as often as you would like to. The same is true for all of the pictures that exist in this room.

When you have seen all you want to see, and when you feel comfortable, slowly start coming back to the awareness of your chair. Feel the gradual change as you become more aware that you are in the room, aware and present, remembering all that you have experienced. Now open your eyes. Write down your experiences as soon as possible. This meditation is a terrific source of information that you might want to write down while it is still fresh in your mind.

Karma and Kinship

A lifetime is as short a journey as that of a drop of water falling over the edge of a cliff. There are an infinite variety of experiences made available to each of us, with only one catch: we are not able to keep anything that we acquire in life, with very few exceptions, one being karma and another being kinship. These are two aspects of being that are not material, and do carry over from one lifetime to the next.

Karma (meaning "deed" in Sanskrit) is a cycle of action and reaction to our every movement in life. It is an energetic force that pulls life together as it attempts to break away. It leaves us with a residue of every action that we have made in life, and requires that we further react in a way to resolve those past actions. We enter into each lifetime with past life karma to resolve, and we create new karma with every step that we take.

For example, if a person was ostracized in a past life for being different in any way, and shunned from their peers or even their family, they will come into the next life with an imprint of that experience. It may be that no matter how nice their new family is, or how much love they are given, they always feel somewhat separate and alone. Karma is undone in the same way that it is done, through opposing experiences that resolve the karmic imprint over time.

Kinship is an energetic bond that all human beings possess. There is a resonant energy in our bodies that oscillates back and forth, grounding us to the earth and reaching up toward the sky, and which contains a powerful magnetic quality. This resonance strengthens the connection we have to our experiences in life, and more importantly, to the family and friends that we share our experiences with. The key is to see that we are powerfully connected to everything and everyone in life by this resonant energy. The more energy we put into a relationship the stronger our resonant energy of kinship will become.

When my son was three years old, he asked me a profound question: "How will I find you when you die?" The great Indian sage Ramana Maharshi was asked the same question when his body was close to death. His response was, "Where will I go?" The question being asked is from the perspective of the mind, and the answer being given is from that of God and truth.

If we approach this question from a path of mind, our answer must be that we will never see each other again. This is because the mind is finite, with a beginning and ending, and the personality that has been created through the mind will die with the body. From this perspective, there is no life after death, which is absolutely true for the mind and personality.

If we approach this question from the path of God, our answer is that we will always be together. We are never apart. Our very beings are connected in every way imaginable. We know that space and time are an illusion. There is nowhere to go. From this perspective, we are able to acknowledge the resonant energy of kinship that continues to bring us together from one lifetime to the next.

Just as it may seem unnecessary from a perspective of mind to ask the question, "How will I wake up in the morning", so too does it seem unnecessary from the perspective of God to ask the question, "How will I find you when you die?"

A Circular Relationship

We run from fear, right into the arms of desire, through what is a circular relationship that keeps us striving for one desirable experience after the next, endlessly. We may never come to realize that our entire way of life is built upon this relationship to fear and desire, because it is set in at a very young age.

In childhood, we begin to experience a sense of separation. This natural sense of separation leads us to identify with the conditions of our body, and thus we start to believe in our own mortality. Every condition of the body that reflects its own mortality, such as a wound, virus, or disease, strengthens the fear of death.

We quickly learn that the fear of death is alleviated, only momentarily, by attaining something that we desire. We learn the art of suppressing and avoiding all forms of fear, because it seems difficult to accept and transform them. Instead, as a distraction from having to face our own fears, we focus our attention and energy on ways to obtain that which we desire.

This cycle of running from what we fear, towards that which we desire is due to a simple misunderstanding of our relationship to life. It comes from the belief that we are in this world and of this world – that we are this body, mind, and the sum total of its experiences. But we are not. The deeper we realize this truth, the more we are able to break free from the cycle of fear and desire.

∞ 24 ∞

Practice Idea: Acceptance Affirmations

"Accept yourself, all of yourself . . . That which you resist, persists!"

~Carl Jung

Many aspects of being human, such as having fear and desire, are blessings in disguise when we learn to embrace them. Since our own true nature embraces all forms of experience, the more we are able to love and accept ourselves and our lives, the closer we come to knowing our authentic self.

An affirmation is any thought that we have or word we say which reflects our inner truth, and helps lead us to the choices we make in each moment. An acceptance affirmation is usually a short statement targeted at a challenging set of beliefs that have been previously difficult for us to accept. Think of this exercise as a way of simply giving yourself permission to embrace more of your life in a positive way.

Start by taking a moment to think about areas of your life that have been difficult to accept. Write the most important ones down in a list. Now look at each item on the list and write out a few positive statements for each. They need to be positive and in the present tense, and focused on what you want to be able to accept. For example:

If I have a difficult time accepting:

Who I am

My acceptance affirmation might be:

I love and accept myself

If I have a difficult time accepting:

My life

My acceptance affirmation might be:

I accept and appreciate the
life I have created for myself

If I have a difficult time accepting:

Change in my life

My acceptance affirmation might be:

I accept and release everything in my
life that is beyond my power to change

Keep in mind that acceptance affirmations are only as powerful as the effort we make to repeat them throughout our day. You can say, sing, or chant them to yourself or out loud. The amount of time that it takes for the affirmation to sink in and have an effect on your life depends upon the strength of the message you are trying to embrace.

"Everyone is a mirror image of yourself - your own thinking coming back to you . . . Come to see that everything outside you is a reflection of your own thinking. You are the storyteller, the projector of all stories, and the world is the projected image of your thoughts."

~Byron Katie

5

Thoughts, Stories, and Projections

Enlightenment is the freedom of experiencing life without attachment to any thought, story, or projection that arises within your own mind. When you are able to see through each of these, no individual sense of "me" is created – there is no ego. There is nothing to believe in, and no one to do the believing. When you see through the game of life, you see that anything that is relatively true is actually false . . . and you are left with the absolute truth, as it unfolds in each and every moment. Now you can reach deeply into God's territory to actualize pure wisdom and intent.

Our minds are like powerful reflective mirrors. They reflect personal aspects of our own experiences. We can become entirely convinced that our own thoughts, stories, and projections are true, because they contain some aspects of truth, and we have the amazing ability to exaggerate any aspect of truth over that which is false – often referred to as my perspective.

"My perspective" as far as thoughts, stories, and projections are concerned only allows one to perceive what is relatively true. Seeing through your own belief in a relative truth is like pulling out a sword and cutting down what is known to be false. This sword of truth is what ends the cycle of experiencing life as being either heaven or hell.

My teacher once said that the belief in a single thought is what sets apart heaven from hell – regardless of whether it is a positive or a negative thought. A positive thought can bring on a heavenly experience, while a negative thought can bring on one of hell. But both are illusions that we can see through and choose to not succumb to. This may seem like a daunting task at first, but seeing through one belief naturally leads to doing the same with the next, until we find that we are doing so in each and every moment.

What We Call Ego

The most important thing to realize is that you are not who you believe yourself to be. You are not your ego. What we call ego does not actually exist, and what does not exist cannot really live. The ego is only imagined. It is a powerful commentary that we take along for the ride.

Think of it like this: in Santa Cruz, Ca there is an amusement park that has a ride called *The Cave Train Adventure*. You board a miniature train that enters into a prehistoric cave filled with dinosaurs and Neanderthals set in amusing scenes.

There is a tour guide on the ride, who pretends to drive the train while commenting on each scene; basically, the tour guide performs a task similar to that of the ego. Neither one is in control, but they both act as if they are. They both have knowledge and familiarity with almost every aspect of the experience. It seems as if they know exactly what is going to happen next, and they do to some extent, because they are bound to a circular track that repeats the same scenes over and over again. This is precisely what we call ego.

The Egoic Rhythm

Rhythm is an essential aspect of life. The sun rises and sets each new day. The seasons come and go every year. We wake up and fall asleep to the physical world. These are just a few of the natural rhythms that have had an effect on the evolution of human consciousness.

Our minds are oriented toward thinking in rhythmic patterns. We think in terms of cause and effect, action and reaction. Our conditioning, from the time of birth to the present moment, is often supported by the reinforcement of one action over another. This conditioning sets our thoughts into an egoic rhythm that leads to the formation of an individual and personal ego.

The ego, who we think we are, is simply a conditioned rhythm of thoughts, stories, and projections that we believe. There is a general timeline in which we can see the ego being formed and strengthened through the rhythm of our lives.

From around birth to the age of three: an early sense of self develops. Children are conditioned to think of life in terms of *me* and *you*, *mine* and *yours*, *my* turn and *your* turn. When a child falls down and gets hurt, they begin to think of the pain as being *my* pain, not *your* pain.

From the age of three to around seven: a little ego develops out of the early sense of self. The little ego begins to stick because children start to connect thoughts with feelings. A certain thought begins to feel a certain way in the body. They are already conditioned to understand that *my* thoughts belong to *me*, and so do *my* feelings.

From the age of seven to around thirteen: The ego is strengthened through a sense of who *I* am in the world. This is how *I* feel. That is what *I* think. Now *I* am going to act. All of which is in relationship to the rest of life. There is a stronger sense of *me* in a social context.

From the age of thirteen to close to eighteen: the ego becomes solidified. A basic rhythm of thought in response to life has taken over. It has been tested and reinforced through many different contexts. This is the basic personality structure that will be refined throughout the rest of one's life.

From sometime around the age of eighteen on: the ego takes the show on the road. There is a strong sense of self in relationship to the rest of life that moves out into the world through every experience.

There is absolutely nothing wrong with the ego structure. It is actually very healthy to have a strong ego or sense of self at these stages in life. At some point, in the process of maturing, many of these ego structures fall away on their own, because they no longer serve a purpose.

As these structures begin to fall away, we may experience a gap in the rhythm of our thoughts, stories, and projections. We start to realize that we are not the persona that we have constructed and believed ourselves to be. This gap can be great enough to create an actual disruption in the egoic rhythm. This is commonly referred to as a midlife crisis. A midlife crisis is actually a form of awakening. Some people have this experience in their twenties, while others have it in their sixties. There is no predicting when the egoic rhythm will lose its strength, or if its strength will be renewed.

A natural tendency of seeing through the ego structure is to reject it. We may realize that the ego is *not me* and attempt to get rid of it like our bodies would a virus, but this is just more ego. It is the ego trying to get rid of the ego. Also, there are a number of reasons why we may not choose to continue to see through the egoic rhythm. The more we look, the more we realize that nothing in life is actually real. This can be scary for those of us who are still relatively identified with our experiences.

Befriend your ego. Learn its secrets. See how it works so that you can see through it. In truth, the ego is something quite beautiful and amazing. There is wisdom in seeing its purpose. The whole game changes when we see that life is just an illusion; smoke and mirrors. The more we look the more we see that it is not actually appearing to and falling away from "me", but from God. This rhythm is God's rhythm, breathing life in and releasing it out, in the present moment.

∞ 29 ∞

Practice Idea: Observe Your Mind

This is a very simple mental exercise. Sit down, close your eyes and observe your mind. The only work that is required here is to become accustomed to being a passive observer of your own mind. Just watch whatever comes and goes without getting involved in any way. Try not to judge what you are watching or do anything with what you observe. It is as simple as that.

Notice that you, the observer, are separate from what you observe. You are separate from the thoughts that occur in your mind. Learning this skill of separating yourself from your own surface thoughts is the intention of this exercise.

The purpose of observing your mind is also to allow all of the endless thoughts, which only persist because you are not aware of them, to be observed, so that they can stop occurring. At some point, the mind chatter will likely slow to a halt, and you will notice that your body is beginning to relax and let go of the stress or anxiety that was being produced by the mind chatter.

Stuck In a Story

Everything that we experience through our five senses is an object of our own perception. When two people view the same object, they may perceive different aspects of it. They may see it from different perspectives.

If two people are looking at a ball that appears to be striped to the person standing on one side and polka-dotted to the person standing on the other side, then these two people will have a very different experience of the same object. They will describe the ball differently. They might even have a debate over who has the right perspective. Some people call this "arguing for your limitations".

There is a common tendency to create a story or projection around our perspectives. For instance, the first person could say, "I was looking at a ball that was obviously striped, but every time I described it to the other person they insisted that it was not. I felt like I was going insane!" We are persuaded to believe in these stories by the very egoic voice that created them, and so they continue to evolve and become more and more sophisticated. As they evolve, we also infuse them with our own emotions. In this sense, we breathe life into our stories and projections. This is what makes us master storytellers.

Our stories are everything from simple to complicated, naïve to sophisticated, tragic to blessed, and so on. Every story is personal. The better the story, the more believable it is – the better the distraction. We become distracted from seeing the truth that what we perceive and what we believe are only a story. At some point, we may become aware that we are telling a story and believing in it fully. This awareness cuts right through the story and all of its related projections. It is like turning a light on in a movie theater, making it extremely difficult to reengage the story. The story will most likely continue to play out in the background, but it will no longer seem real. We can now see the story for what it is, because we have gained yet another perspective, that of awareness itself. The story has become a more distant and abstract object within our overall field of awareness.

Cogito Ergo Sum

Cogito ergo sum (meaning "I think, therefore I am" in Latin) is the existential statement made by the French philosopher René Descartes. It means that if "I" am wondering if "I" exist, the proof is simply in the fact that "I" am having the thought. The implication is that noticing that "I" am the one having thought is enough to prove one's own existence.

This is a tremendous philosophy in terms of gaining distance from one's own thoughts, stories, and projections, because it points back to oneself as being the invisible "I" who is aware of the sensation of thoughts. However, the philosophy falls short in that thinking has absolutely nothing to do with existing. We can prove this in less than ten seconds, by using a mindfulness technique known as the ten-second count.

Close your eyes. Focus all of your attention on your breathing. Put all of your awareness and willpower into each breath as you inhale and exhale. Now slowly count to ten. If your mind wanders to a thought at any point during the count, start over. You can do this until you are able to count to ten without having a single thought. Now open your eyes.

Notice that this invisible "I" not only exists in the absence of thought, but it actually feels more alive and resonant when you are not giving your energy to a thought. The ten-second count is a mindfulness technique that allows the "I" to become present and aware of its own existence outside the realm of thought. The "I" is just another sign or symbol used to represent the authentic self.

Our intent is to acknowledge that the authentic self is always present in the existence and absence of thought. Your authentic self can always become more conscious and mindful of thoughts as they occur, the resultant emotions they produce, and the actions that inevitably follow. There is a pause in between each thought, story, and projection that is like the pause in between each breath. The trick is to become so mindful of these pauses that we no longer need to use any techniques.

∞ 🦢 ∞

Practice Idea: Being Mindful

Here is another simple exercise that can be done anytime throughout the day. Start by looking at your watch and noting the time. For the next 60 seconds you want to focus all your attention on your breathing.

Although it is only one minute, it may feel like an eternity. Keep your eyes open and breathe normally. Be alert. If your mind begins to wander, simply return your attention to your breath.

Mindfulness cues: Try adding mindfulness cues to this exercise. Whenever an environmental cue occurs, such as seeing your reflection in a mirror, promptly bring your attention into the present moment and stay focused on your breath for sixty seconds. Simply choose a cue that works for you to further integrate mindfulness into all aspects of your daily life.

Labyrinth of Thought

The only way out is through. There is no way to permanently avoid or escape from the endless labyrinth of thought. We can only bypass, meditate around, or ignore it for so long – just long enough to get a taste of the authentic self – before the actual energy of thought, which continues to build as it is being held back, is released once again through the mind.

These thoughts are like a child that acts out for attention. Ignoring the child might bring you some peace for a while, and bribery is another short-lived solution. However, if we take the approach of trying to understand why the child is acting out, we may just find a lasting remedy.

Seeing through the game of life is the knowing that the chatter of mind that we listen to is really hit or miss as far as reflecting the truth of any moment. We often entertain our own opinions and judgments, which most of us can laugh at; our own fears and desires, which we have some sense of perspective about; but how often do we make an effort to truly understand why this endless labyrinth of thought is playing out and why we engage it from such an unconscious awareness? Let's befriend our thoughts. Let's get to know them. Let's look at them with the intention of really seeing how and why we view the world as we do. One way to do this is by journaling.

When we record our thoughts by journaling (or by creating an audio file), our thoughts are placed outside of us, and can be more readily examined. Take a moment to practice journaling some thoughts. Try to think of an experience that you had today and write about it. You may have had a cup of coffee with a friend, received some kind of news, or talked shop with a co-worker. Simply reflect upon the experience and record any thoughts, feelings, or reactions that you had.

Once you are done recording the moment, put it aside. It does little good to review a thought from the same perspective you were in when it was recorded. Like adding water to a glass of water, there will be little difference other than volume. By placing it aside, you can allow yourself to have enough distance to return to it as an outsider looking in.

Once you feel that enough time has passed for this distance to be achieved, review it. Examine it. Analyze it. See what it means to you from the perspective of being detached from it. The most important thing to remember is that by journaling past events, we gain awareness of our recurring thoughts, stories, and projections. This awareness can ultimately free us from repeating the same choices that lead to the same outcomes.

To Project or Reflect

A common mistake that most of us make when searching for aspects of our true nature such as wisdom, compassion, and peace, is to think that it will come from the mind. But peace does not come from the mind, nor does compassion or wisdom. These are not aspects of the mind. The mind's purpose is simply to *project* or *reflect*.

The mind can be used to *project* a powerful image of what we want to create, hold onto that image, and actualize it. Our projections are often determined by who we believe ourselves to be. If I believe myself to be an athlete, meaning that my mind projects the thoughts of an athlete, I will likely manifest the circumstances that lead to having a fit body. The mind can also be used to *reflect* upon a past experience, and compare or analyze the difference between what happened then and what we want to have happen now or in the future.

The mind is a powerful tool that can be used to further develop areas of industry, such as agriculture, construction, government, healthcare, manufacturing, and technology; but it falls short when applied toward relating to and knowing one's self and others. It leaves us feeling isolated and separated from each other and from life, by creating a veil of past reflections of thought that we simply cannot see through. This veil of thought becomes a story, and we project onto every subsequent experience.

This is the human dilemma. It has been happening for so long, and largely without question, that it is now our predominant way of life. With careful observation, we can become conscious of our past reflections, and learn how to use them appropriately. It is entirely within our capacity to do so. We know this to be true in moments when everything seems to fall into place, when every aspect of our experience is working together – when there is a right fit, and everything seems to click.

The before and after experiences of these two different ways of being are startling. Before, caught in a veil of reflective thoughts, stories, and projections, we feel like busy bees trying to see through a wall of honey; after, seeing through the veil, we feel like fish swimming in a calm sea of water. The difference is both surprising and undeniable.

The Buddhist practice of mindfulness is a systematic study of the mind that is designed to help us observe these differences. It is the practice of watching the mind and taking note of its qualities and attributes. By paying close attention to our own thoughts we can become more mindful of how they work. Our intention is to allow all states of being to exist in their rightful place, so that we can be free to move in life without any self-imposed hindrances.

Proof by Assertion

A lie repeated often enough can become one's truth. A thought repeated often enough can become one's reality. This form of logic is known as "proof by assertion". When a thought, story, or projection is repeated and there are no contradictions, it can be accepted as one's own truth.

Thoughts are not real. They do not exist. Thoughts are produced by a movement of energy in the brain. Energy is real and measurable, but thoughts themselves are not. We believe our thoughts to be real and true all the time. Why? Without the experience of the authentic self or true nature, there is nothing to contradict the thoughts, stories, and projections that are constantly repeated within the mind. In the absence of contradiction, they become one's truth and reality. Think of the expression "seeing is believing". Reality is thought to be a certain way, until we see something that contradicts this.

A positive thought can create a pleasant reality, while a negative thought can create a troublesome reality. Neither one is real or true. They are both an illusion. The moon presents the illusion of being a source of light when it is truly reflecting the light of the sun, just as our thoughts present the illusion of being reality when they are really a partial reflection of the whole truth. Seeing this contradiction is enough to break the power we have given to our thoughts. It is like having a key that unlocks the door to our own freedom.

A single thought creates division, because you are the subject perceiving an object of thought. The more energy you give to thought, the more you will feel divided. The less energy you give to thought, the more you will feel connected. There is a tendency to get so caught up in your thoughts that you miss what is happening right in front of you.

You can look at your computer while thinking about an email that was just sent. You can put on an old pair of shoes while thinking about the new pair of shoes you are going to buy. These examples illustrate a common theme of division. A single thought can divide your attention and keep you from seeing what is right in front of you.

It is this habit of mind that creates the difference between being a seeker of truth, and a knower of truth. A seeker of truth has had some deep insight, and thinks about that experience as they move through life. The seeker of truth might look at the leaves of a tree and think about how we are all connected to God in the same way that the leaves are connected to the tree. A knower of truth will look at the leaves without much ado, and have a full-blown experience of God and connection.

Be a knower of truth, not a seeker of truth. Know that a lie repeated often enough to become one's truth is still a lie. Wisdom knows this difference. It is what ultimately sets us free in each and every moment.

∞ ⟨⟩ ∞

Practice Idea: Beginner's Mind

"Concentrate on a single thought: Concentrating on one thought, all other thoughts disappear; finally that thought also disappears."

~Ramana Maharshi

This technique is an excellent approach to entering into a state that Zen Buddhists refer to as the beginner's mind. Zen master Shunryu Suzuki once said that "in the beginner's mind there are many possibilities, in the expert's mind there are few." When we direct our awareness inwardly, not taking notice of any mind chatter, and place all of our attention on a pre-chosen thought or idea, we can exhaust that thought and enter into a state of beginner's mind.

This is a state of no-mind, or emptiness, where our awareness is resting in the powerful silence that exists in the absence of thought. This empty silence is completely open and aware. It is a source of wisdom and power within ourselves that we have access to at all times.

Thought-Feeling Connection

Many years ago, I took an old friend on a road trip from Santa Cruz to San Luis Obispo, Ca. My friend had Parkinson's disease, and we often went on little trips to support his peace of mind. One night, in a little villa that we had rented, I was suddenly awakened by an intense sound of snoring that came from his room – a condition related to the Parkinson's disease. The sound seemed to echo and amplify across the entire villa.

It startled me awake. I remember thinking, "You have got to be kidding me. This is not okay. It must be two in the morning." At the same time that these thoughts occurred to me, I noticed that my body was in a deep state of relaxation. It felt happy and content. It was so sweet to be in my body at that moment.

There was a vast difference between my thoughts and feelings. When I noticed this difference, it became nearly impossible for me to continue to have agitated thoughts. My feelings just would not support them. I felt way too relaxed and content to have such thoughts. This is when I realized the powerful connection between my thoughts and feelings.

Our feelings breathe life into our thoughts. They give power to our thoughts. Without feeling an emotional connection to our thoughts, they will fall short every time. They will look plain and uninteresting, and we will not be motivated to act them out, which represent yet another moment of what life holds for us when we are seeing through the game.

"Mysticism is: a. An advanced state of inner enlightenment. b. Union with Reality. c. A state of genuinely satisfying success. d. Insight into an entirely new world of living. e. An intuitive grasp of Truth, above and beyond intellectual reasoning. f. A personal experience, in which we are happy and healthy human beings."

~Vernon Howard

6

Mystical Experiences

Seeing through the game of life is a path of awakening to your authentic self, where you will encounter many unfamiliar experiences that we call mystical, and you will become skilled at using mystical tools. There can be a tendency to fixate on these powerful new experiences and tools, rather than allow your path to continue to unfold. Just let go. Allow the many twists and turns to occur. It is important to be open and explorative, and to approach every mystical experience from a place of honesty and integrity.

Some people are more inclined toward having mystical experiences than others. A mystical experience can be anything from seeing the true nature of a flower to having a conversation with God. For most people, mystical experiences naturally occur on their own, if we are open to receiving them. They can be, and usually are, easily dismissed as something like déjà vu or intuition. Yet if these experiences are cultivated with wisdom, intent, and purpose they can be transformative and add to the richness of our lives.

One way to cultivate mystical experience is to find another person who is steeped in these mysteries. If you are a light healer, resonating with another light healer can reinforce and amplify your skills. You can work with a friend or teacher, either someone who is alive or who exists in the inner world. Their designation really does not matter – only that together you are working with your mystical tools in a positive way.

An endless number of mystical experiences can and will arise if we are open to them, such as bliss, astral travel, timelessness, spacelessness, oneness, nothingness, channeling, healing, light and sound resonance, and vision or foresight. When a new mystical tool has been made available, there is a tendency to shift our gaze away from the unfolding process of self-realization, and to instead hyper focus on strengthening our newest area of interest. We are likely to identify with it as a way of being in the world. We call ourselves light healers, channelers, psychics and so on.

It is important to realize that these new tools came from mystical experiences that naturally arose, like all other experiences. They can be a pleasure to observe and cultivate, but there is absolutely no need to fixate on them, or to identify with them. The unfolding process of self-realization is what brought these mystical experiences and tools, and if they are to continue to play an important part in our lives, they will naturally occur on their own.

These experiences profoundly change the way we think about ourselves and life, and the way we choose to be in the world. They can feel so powerful and overwhelming at times that we may attempt to shut them out, or we may walk away out of fear. It is important to be able to talk about these experiences, so that if and when this fear arises, we can immediately process it and continue to move forward. As we continue to allow this process to unfold, we discover that it is both safe and natural to have mystical experiences on a continuous basis.

Being Gifted

Human beings are reflections of God. We are highly sophisticated creations that are the reflection of a highly sophisticated creator. We are not the byproducts of chance. It stands to figure that our lessons in life are also not a byproduct of chance, but the practice of cultivating skills and talents that reflect God to a greater extent.

The skills and talents that seem to have come naturally to us since birth were actually developed in past lifetimes. This is why some children have a naturally greater ability to do things like play music, perform experiments, or philosophize about life. These past life talents serve as a natural foundation for this lifetime. They can be very useful if we know how to bring them out of our unconsciousness.

We could be using hundreds of past life talents right now, if you only knew how to have access to them. We want to call upon this valuable experience, and make it a conscious part of our daily lives. Let's not lose so much of our potential to be great and to have great lives, because we are stuck in the mindset of only having *one life to live.*

∞ 𝓛𝓳 ∞

Practice Idea: Past Life Talents

The first step in becoming conscious of your past life talents is to ask yourself why you have chosen to be closed off to these talents up until now. You may have blocked your access to these talents for a reason. It is quite possible that in a past life you misused the skill, or it could be that you believe accessing it may divert you from your present life goals. Whatever the case may be, to uncover your past life talents you will need to be honest and open to receiving any information that arises.

Begin with being comfortable. Find a quiet and relaxing place to sit or lie down for ten minutes or so. Take a few deep breaths. Close your eyes and imagine a pool of water. See yourself walking toward the pool of water. Place both hands upon the surface of the water and notice that it seems to reflect a special quality of silver and white light. You feel safe and protected. There is a sense of connecting to a great mystery that is full of wisdom and life.

Now say to yourself: *I wish to reclaim the talents, skills, and abilities from my past lives that will further the progress of my current life. I am open to receiving these gifts and having them brought into my life.*

Imagine seeing a reflection of angelic hands within the pool of water. The hands are holding symbols of your past life talents, such as a brush for the talent of painting or an instrument for that of music. Know that these talents are those that will best serve you in this life. If you decide to receive these gifts, reach into the water and accept and embrace them with your entire being, until they are within you. If you do not wish to accept these gifts at this time, let them remain within the pool of water – where they will stay until you decide to reclaim them. When there is no longer a reflection of the angelic hands, you will know that the process is complete. Say the words "So be it" in acceptance, open your eyes, and return to your life.

It may take some time to reconnect with your past life talents as they naturally and effortlessly come to light in your day-to-day life. You will notice a sense of unlearned knowledge with what you are doing that is related to your past life talents. These gifts will remain with you as long as they continue to serve you in your present life.

Present Awareness

There is no time like the present moment, for it is all that we ever truly have. We are always present. There is no way to be any more or less present than we already are. It only takes a single thought, *I am not present*, to imagine, believe, and therefore experience otherwise, but this does not change the fact that we are still present in imagining that we are not.

Human beings have two predominant states of awareness that exist in the present moment: *expansive awareness*, and *contracted awareness*. *Expansive awareness* is an experience of oneness with everything that you are aware of. It is a lightness of being that happens within the framework of your body. You may feel slightly lifted up out of your body, or completely out of your body, but remember that both experiences are just different sensations that are occurring within your own body and mind.

You may have an experience that is so expansive that it encompasses the area around your house, street, city, state, country, or even the world. Your awareness can expand to the point that you sense that the entire universe is somehow within your own body.

When I was a child, I often had the experience of expansive awareness. I felt like I was flying around my bedroom, looking down at myself, yet somehow feeling the experience from within my little body. It was a wonderful time in life. One day the experience simply stopped happening, and I remember thinking, *did that really happen or was I just imagining it?*

All I knew was that something had changed. My body and mind felt more solid and tangible. I was almost instantly identified with any thought or feeling that occurred to me. It was not a conscious shift, but one that seemed to reflect the inherent nature of my environment. Through repeated conditioning, I entered into a state of *contracted awareness*, where I remained for nearly two decades.

I was mostly unconscious of any shifts that I made between expansive and contracted awareness, until I was close to twenty-three years old, when I was given the opportunity to attend a silent retreat with a true spiritual teacher. On this retreat, my awareness expanded and I once again experienced the lightness of being in a state of oneness. It was then that I remembered my childhood experience, and understood how I had come to feel trapped within my own body and mind.

Although we may try to be in a state of expansive awareness all the time, it is natural to return to a state of contracted awareness. Both experiences serve different purposes, and will come and go on their own. As we learn to access these states of awareness, it becomes as natural to watch them move on their own as it is to watch our thoughts come and go.

Path of the Heart

Think of the symbol commonly associated with Jesus: the symbol of a heart on fire. In Gaelic or Sufi traditions this symbol has been depicted as a heart with wings. This is to symbolize the very real experience of having one's heart opened up.

Your heart has the capacity to be open or closed. This is one of the ways you interpret information through your body. You may not even realize that your heart is closed until it is ripped wide open. This is what it means to have your heart on fire.

In my case, it happened quite spontaneously. In my twenties, I entered into a state of expansive awareness, and heard an inner voice say, "You are free." A sensation of light and heat grew within my chest. I saw the image of powerful wings spreading out from my own heart. A flame suddenly engulfed this symbol, and I fell to my knees with the sensation of fire running throughout my chest. The pain was searing and raw. Tears streamed from my eyes. My heart was miraculously ripped wide open.

This is a path my heart needed to take to allow me to become more aware of my true nature. The heart knows love to be an inherent aspect of our authentic self. True love exists without purpose or meaning. It can be felt deeply in one's own heart.

I have since learned that the opening of one's heart does not need to occur miraculously – it can be initiated. You can open your heart by initiating an experience of expansive awareness in your body. Your body is a constant reminder that you are always present. Your heart beats now. Your blood pulses now. Your lungs expand and contract now. If you focus all of your attention on a single one of these aspects of your body, you will inevitably enter into a state of expansive awareness.

From the state of expansive awareness, a sensation of energy will grow in your body. You may feel a slight tingling in your feet or hands. A sensation of energy will occur somewhere in your body. Wherever it occurs, focus all of your attention there, and the energy will grow and spread to other places in your body. When you feel this energy within the area of your heart, bring every ounce of your attention to it. The sensation may feel faint at first, but it will surely grow. Be patient. Allow it to become saturated and full.

At this point, you will have your own heart-opening experience. It may be a faint experience, or a profound one, depending upon where you are in your own journey. Once your heart is open, try moving around in the world, seeing what it is like to experience life with an open heart.

The Sound and Light Currents

The sound and light currents have been referred to as the *word* of God. The word of God is life itself. It is creation. The sound and light currents are two components of creation that spontaneously arise from God. The vibration of sound and light can be heard and seen in meditation through an inner sense. Through intuition we sense the sound and light currents to be a sacred energy contained within all aspects of life.

The sound current is a resonant, interwoven vibration of energy. It is the sound of particles in motion, of creation and destruction. It strengthens our perception of life. It gives body and flavor to the vision of life that is created through the light current.

The sound current can be accessed by placing your awareness upon a single sound. Focus on a natural sound that comes from the rain, fire, wind, or earth. Listen to the wind, feel it resonate, and allow your body to connect and move with the energy. The energetic sound will resonate and connect with other energetic sounds. These connections weave in and out of each other like a beautiful symphony. It may occur to you that you are hearing the sound of angels singing. If you continue to connect with this symphony of resonant sound, your awareness will return to the source of creation.

The light current is a radiant white light. Without light, there is only darkness. The light current separates night from day. This combination gives us the sensory perception of change, through which our mental perception of time and space are conceived. The light current itself does not contain any darkness. It has the power to transmute the darkness into light. It is the source of absolute wisdom and truth.

The light current is the light of awareness. It reveals the true nature of our existence, and is present in every experience. We can connect to it by simply meditating upon an object. All forms of light, such as firelight, sunlight, inner-light, and even electricity are expressions of the resonant energy of the light current.

The key to seeing the light current through an object is being able to calm your mind. With a calm mind, you may notice that an object seems to emit a bit more light. It will appear to be a little more crisp and clear. Your intuitive sense of the light will be drawn to the object like a moth to a flame.

The light will grow in brilliance, until you see it all around you, permeating everyone and everything. The experience is a blessing. If you stay with the blessing, it too will take you back to the source of creation.

∞ ⚕ ∞

Practice Idea: Chanting HU or AUM

HU (pronounced "Hue") and AUM (pronounced "Om") are ancient Sanskrit names for God. They encompass every tone and every sound in existence. Chanting HU or AUM allows us to move beyond our thoughts and feelings, through a spiritual tone or vibration that connects us to the energy that flows directly from God throughout all of life. It helps us overcome our apparent limitations and move into the grace of God. As our awareness of HU or AUM develops we begin to resonate with the sound of creation and also experience the light of God.

For the purpose of this exercise, we will use a variation of the HU chant, ANI-HU (pronounced "ahn-eye-hue"; meaning *empathy with God*). This chant is a way of invoking God with the added dimension of bringing a quality of empathy and oneness with others.

Find a quiet and comfortable place to sit. Close your eyes. Call yourself forward into the light for the highest good, and ask for protection and guidance. Chant the sacred word ANI-HU inwardly, silently.

While chanting, focus your awareness on the area near the center of your head, directly back from your forehead. This is one area where your being rests and gathers energy, commonly referred to as "the seat of the soul". After you have chanted for close to five minutes, stop and listen within. You are listening for a very subtle vibration of energy known as the sound current.

The great Indian spiritual master Paramahansa Yogananda likened the sound current to a "cosmic symphony of all vibratory sound," like the "melodic strain of the humming of bees, the tone of a flute, a harp, a bell-like sound." It may take some time and practice before you are able to hear or recognize the sound current.

If your mind begins to wander or you lose the focus of listening, simply bring your awareness back to chanting again. Try to follow every five-minute interval of listening with another five-minute interval of chanting. The idea is to alternate between chanting and listening.

If you see a purple, golden, silver, or white light you can allow yourself to follow this inwardly. These colors are indications of elevated states of consciousness assumed by the energy from the highest source of light and sound as it awakens us through the awareness of our being.

After about five more minutes, you can open your eyes. Bring your awareness and energy back into your body by gently moving your fingers and toes. Through daily practice you can gradually increase the amount of time that you are in this exercise.

Energetic Resonance

Atoms are the basic building blocks of life. Everything in life consists of these very tiny particles. An atom is made up of mostly empty space and a few subatomic particles. There is enough energy in one atom to lift a can of soda four inches off the ground. A single person has over $7*10^{27}$ atoms in their body. That is, 7 followed by 27 zeros, which is the energetic equivalent to over thirty-five hydrogen bombs.

There are a few basic ways that we can recharge the energy in our bodies. We can do so through sunlight, oxygen, and food, and by accessing what is often referred to as life force. The empty space that exists within each atom is life force. It is a bond that holds our entire universe together. It is a mysterious force that is just beginning to be seen in the field of quantum physics.

Life force can be likened to the energy that one receives when they enter into a state of silence. The emptiness or silence that we perceive and are energized by in meditation is the same life force that exists as empty space within an atom. We have access to this energy at all times.

Several years ago, in meditation, I learned how to access this life force for myself. With my eyes closed, in a deep state of silence, I noticed a current of energy running throughout my body. As I placed my awareness on this energy it was instantly strengthened and renewed. It grew and became more powerful and resonant.

This life force is a transference of energy: chemical, thermal, electric, luminous, and radiant energy that surges in, out, and through your body and everything else that you are aware of. You can feel it stimulating the electrical and chemical impulses in your brain – all of which lead to a heightened sense of light, sound, and intuition . . . strengthening our capacity to see through the game of life.

Just as our bodies can be physically thrown out of alignment, so can they be energetically thrown out of alignment. Through the practice of meditation and other energy healing techniques, the power of life force can be used to restore our bodies and minds to a natural state of balance.

The essential goals of all energy healing techniques are to see where we are out of alignment, cleanse our energetic fields, and direct them toward a state of harmony. An energy healing can be performed through techniques such as hands-on-healing, acupuncture, acupressure, Reiki, chi gong, or craniosacral.

By way of meditation and the use of these techniques, we can access and harness our own life force. We can return to a natural state of balance and harmony. Our senses can remain clear, our minds calm and sharp, and life will once again feel alive and enjoyable.

The Inner World

The inner world is often thought of as an unseen dimension that parallels our own existence, but which is not visible in states of ordinary consciousness. Our thoughts and dreams first take shape in the inner world before we bring them into our physical lives.

We can access this realm to connect with pure energy and wisdom, to send or receive healings, to communicate with enlightened beings, or to visit other locations in the universe. An inner projection is the act of sending your consciousness out at will to a location away from your physical body. While this is ultimately a mental projection, it is also a real experience and creates actual phenomena that have a direct impact on one's life.

The physical world is the last plane of existence. Our experiences in the physical world lead us to believe that it is a starting point, but it is really an ending point. We work backwards from the physical world, when entering into the inner world. From the physical world, we can enter into the plane of emptiness. This is a gateway into all planes of existence.

The plane of emptiness is the backdrop of nothingness upon which our physical world and thoughts are projected. It can be easily experienced with our eyes closed. Within the plane of emptiness we are likely to first encounter our own thoughts, stories, and projections. This is a powerful place where we can examine, interpret, and change our patterns of thought. If we are able to release our thoughts, or they cease to arise on their own, we can have the experience of being surrounded by the vibrant ocean of emptiness.

Another plane of existence is the astral plane. In the astral plane we can assume the shape of an astral body, which is also known as a spirit body. It is in this plane of existence that we can connect with pure energy and wisdom, send or receive healings, communicate with other beings, and astral project or travel.

We can enter into the plane of God from any dimension within the inner world, simply by keeping our awareness focused on the backdrop of emptiness. In the plane of God, there is no personal will, sense of separation, or self-concept. You are God. God is you. It is a perfect union.

We unconsciously enter the plane of God every time we go to sleep. When we do so consciously, we perceive a choice as to whether we will remain within God or return to the physical world. If you perceive a sense of compassion or love for the physical world arising within the experience of God, your being is already on its way back to the physical world, which is most often the case.

∞ ② ∞

Practice Idea: Journey Within

Find a quiet room. Sit down in a comfortable position. Close your eyes. Relax. Breathe in deeply, and exhale slowly. With every breath in you are becoming more calm and relaxed, and with every breath out you are releasing anxiety and stress.

Breathe in, and breathe out. As you breathe in, imagine a wave of white light washing over your body, from the tip of your toes to the top of your head. As you breathe out, imagine this wave of white light washing down your back and out the soles of your feet. With every cycle of breath, continue to release any physical or mental stress that you have been carrying. Relax more and more deeply.

Imagine that you are suspended just above your body, looking down at yourself. *(pause)* Now imagine that you are looking down at your body from a distance of ten feet above. *(pause)* Observe your body and the surrounding area from a distance of twenty feet above. *(pause)*

Now set the intention of your inner journey. You may decide to visit another location on our planet, send your presence to another part of the universe, or offer a healing to an ailing person. If any questions arise during your journey, ask them and wait for your authentic self to respond.

You will recognize your authentic self as an image or voice of unequivocal wisdom and clarity. Focus all of your awareness on your authentic self, and merge with it. Now you are in alignment with your authentic self and have access to divine wisdom and strength.

Simply allow the experience to flow into your awareness like a daydream. If you visit a particular planet, ask yourself as many questions as you would like to have answers to. You will be amazed by the knowing that comes out of your awareness when you are in alignment with your authentic self.

Your intuition will tell you when it is time to end the journey within. Simply tell yourself that is it time to return to your body. You will feel yourself moving through the different planes of existence until you move right in to your body. Once you have returned to your body, focus once again on breathing. Breathe in deeply, and breathe out slowly.

Now open your eyes. Notice that you are awake, feel rested and energized, and are in complete alignment with your authentic self. You may want to write down your inner journey while it is fresh in your mind. Any questions that you still have can be asked and answered by your own voice in this state of perfect alignment with your authentic self.

Bridging the Gap

Every single experience in life is a mystical one, divine and mysterious. Regardless of whether we use tea leaves to access our intuition or to simply make a nice warm drink – both are mystical experiences; both are godly. This can be seen clearly when we set aside our disbeliefs and see through our own conditioning and points of view.

There are as many paths to enlightenment as there are philosophies of thought – each having their own apparent sense of difference; each requiring its own form of resolution. In truth, there is no real gap, between these different paths, to bridge. We need only to see through each unique pattern of thought. A rigid perspective may require a more resolute path to assist in seeing through it; whereas, an easy-going attitude may require a moderate path. Both perspectives can be broken down accordingly, and reveal the exact same awareness of truth.

"In truth everyone is a shadow of the Beloved. Our seeking is his seeking. Our words are his words . . . (God) breathes into my ear until my soul takes on his fragrance. He is the soul of my soul. How can I escape? We search for him here and there while looking right at him."

~ Rumi

7

Seeing Through the Game of Life

Seeing through the game of life is the beginning of the self-fulfilling prophecy of enlightenment – the advent of awakening to the authentic self. It is being free from having to play the game of ego: the conditional labyrinth of thoughts, stories, and projections about our lives that reflect a divided way of seeing the world . . . one that keeps us from experiencing our own mystical nature, and the ultimate truth of our existence. Seeing through this game is the beginning of enlightenment, giving rise to a new vision of life – one that is full of wisdom, compassion and grace.

The game of life is what we make of it. Shakespeare once wrote that "All the world's a stage, and all the men and women merely players." Our world is inhabited by nearly seven billion players, each living out their own egoic games. Seeing through these games allows us to fully embrace life.

Seeing through the game of life is the dawn of enlightenment. It is a return to where you have come from, an end to the old ways of being that no longer serve you, and a return to those that are always fresh and new. You are a drop of water and God is the ocean. A cloud, stream, or river will return you to where you have come from. Once you enter into the ocean, you become one with it. The same is also true of seeing through the game of life. Once you see through it, you become one with it. The path is natural, perfect and complete.

∞ ⚉ ∞

Be like a star that has been set afire, continues to blaze, and will shine forever more, always.

~Bodhi Daya

PRACTICE IDEAS FOR
SEEING THROUGH THE GAME OF LIFE

About the Author

Bodhi Daya, author of *Seeing Through the Game of Life* came to the realization of absolute truth through a series of spiritual awakenings that span the course of over a decade. *Seeing Through the Game of Life* is a culmination of the work that he and his wife have done together in this period of time.

∞ ② ∞

The Bodhi Daya Foundation

The Bodhi Daya Foundation is a nonprofit organization founded to support the teachings of absolute truth. It is supported by the efforts of its volunteers and the generous financial contributions of its donors. For more information about the Bodhi Daya Foundation, please visit us at www.bodhidaya.com, or email bodhidaya@gmail.com.

GraceWay Sanctuary Hawaii
Healing Arts Spa & Retreat Center

The Bodhi Daya Foundation is planning to create its first eco-friendly healing arts spa and retreat center to host and support events, seminars, and workshops centered around the teachings of absolute truth - such as those found in *Seeing Through the Game of Life* – a place where you can rest in the light of awareness, relax your body and mind through yoga and meditation; while enjoying the natural elements of earth, wind, fire, and water that help to create a harmonious experience of well-being. We gratefully welcome all donations that are offered to support this endeavor. For more information about GraceWay Sanctuary Hawaii, please visit us online at www.gracewaysanctuary.com.

Section Notes

SECTION ONE

A Brave New World

1. Huxley, Aldous. *Brave New World*. New York: Harper Perenial, 1969.

2. *The New Jerusalem Bible*. Ed. Susan Jones. New York: Doubleday, 1985.

SECTION TWO

The Authentic Self

1. Coelho, Paulo, & Arias, Juan. *Paulo Coelho: Confessions of a Pilgrim*, New York: Harper Collins, 2001.

2. Tolle, Eckhart. A New Earth: Awakening to Your Life's Purpose, New York: Penquin, 2005.

3. Suzuki, Shunryu. Zen *Mind, Beginner's Mind*, New York: Weatherhill, 1970. Print.

4. Adyashanti. *Emptiness Dancing*, Colorado: Sounds True, 2006.

5. Buddha, Gautam. *Fill your mind with compassion,* is a well-known teaching of the Buddha, c. 563-483 BC.

6. Brown, Raymond E. Introduction to the New Testament, New York: Anchor Bible, 1997.

7. Twain, Mark. Letter to George Bainton describing *the difference between the right word and the almost right word*, 1888.

SECTION THREE

A Self-Fulfilling Prophecy

1. Allen, James. *As A Man Thinketh*, James Allen Library, Internet, 1902.

2. Anicius, Boethius. *The serenity prayer is attributed to the well-known Roman philosopher,* c 500 AD.

3. Gandhi, Mahatma, edited by Parvesh, Jag Chander. *Teachings of Mahatma Ghandi*, The Indian Printing Works, 1945.

4. Buddha, Gautam. *The Heart Sutra* is a well-known sutra used in Buddhist ceremonies and teachings. c. 563-483 BC.

SECTION FOUR

The Ultimate Truth

1. Walsch, Neale Donald. *Conversations with God: An Uncommon Dialogue*. ISBN 0-399-14278-9, 1995.

2. Jung, C.G., et al. Man and His Symbols. New York: Dell, 1968.

3. Buddha, Gautam. *The lotus flower held before his disciple Mahakashyapa is a well-known Buddhist teaching.* C. 563-483 BC.

4. Hanh, Thich Nhat. *Living Buddha, Living Christ*, New York: Riverhead Trade, 1997.

5. Jung, C.G., et al. From his talks on Analytic Psychology, c.1960

SECTION FIVE

Thoughts, Stories, and Projections

1. Katie, Byron, & Mitchell, Stephen. *Loving What Is: Four Questions That Can Change Your Life*, New York: Harmony Books, 2002.

2. Descartes, *René, translated by Cottingham, John. Meditations on First Philosophy, in The Philosophical Writings of Descartes vol II, Cambridge University Press, 1984*

3. Maharshi, Ramana. From his "Who Am I" practices. c. 1930.

4. Suzuki, Shunryu. Zen *Mind, Beginner's Mind*, New York: Weatherhill, 1970. Print.

SECTION SIX
Mystical Experiences

1. Vernon, Howard. *The Mystic Path to Cosmic Power*, Colorado: Reward Classics, 1991.

2. Zukav, Gary. *The Seat of the Soul*, New York: Simon & Schuster, 1989.

3. Yogananda, Paramahansa. *Teachings of the cosmic sound current published on the internet*, c. 2012.

SECTION SEVEN
Seeing Through the Game of Life

1. Rumi, Jalaluddin, translated by Barks, Coleman. *The Essential Rumi*, New York: Harper Collins, 1995.

2. Shakespear, William. *Hamlet*, The New Folger Library Shakespeare, 2010.